FROM HIGH HEELS

TO BUNNY SLIPPERS

Also by Christine Conners

Lipsmackin' Backpackin': Lightweight Trail Tested Recipes for Backcountry Trips (Globe Pequot Press, 2000)

Lipsmackin' Vegetarian Backpackin'
(Globe Pequot Press, 2004)

Capital Careers & Personal Development Series

Other titles in this series include the following:

Be Heard the First Time: The Women's Guide to Powerful Speaking by Susan D. Miller, Ph.D., CCC-SLIP

Million Dollar Networking: The Sure Way to Find, Grow and Keep Your Business by Andrea Nierenberg

More Alive with Color: Personal Colors—Personal Style by Leatrice Eiseman

Nonstop Networking: How to Improve Your Life, Luck and Career by Andrea Nierenberg

Now What Do I Do? The Woman's Guide to a New Career by Jan Cannon, Ph.D.

The Power of Handshaking: For Peak Performance Worldwide by Robert E. Brown and Dorothea Johnson

Save 25% when you order any of these and other fine Capital titles from our Web site: www.capital-books.com.

FROM HIGH HEELS
to BUNNY SLIPPERS

Surviving the Transition from Career to Home

Christine Conners, M.A.

Capital Careers & Personal Development

Capital Books, Inc.
Sterling, Virginia

Capital Books, Inc.
P.O. Box 605
Herndon, Virginia 20172-0605

ISBN 10: 1-933102-14-4
ISBN 13: 978-1-933102-14-6 (alk.paper)

Library of Congress Cataloging-in-Publication Data
Conners, Christine.
  From high heels to bunny slippers : surviving the transition from career to home / Christine Conners.-- 1st ed.
     p. cm.
  ISBN 1-933102-14-4 (pbk. : alk. paper)
  1. Stay-at-home mothers. 2. Work and family. 3. Choice (Psychology) 4. Parenting—Psychological aspects. 5. Life change events. I. Title.
  HQ759.46.C66 2006
  306.874'3—dc22
                                          2005031163

Printed in the United States of America on acid-free paper that meets the American National Standards Institute Z39-48 Standard.

First Edition

10 9 8 7 6 5 4 3 2 1

Contents

Acknowledgments

To my husband, Tim—A man of integrity, a wonderful father, and my best friend. Thank you for all of the weekends you spent helping me with this book, and for putting up with a less than perfect home for the past decade so that I could pursue my "hobby" of writing.

To my children—James, Michael, Maria, and David. You have been an endless source of simple wisdom and improbable adventures. I love you.

To my mother—Barbara Naudain. Thank you for giving me life and not taking it back when I was a teenager.

To my publisher—Kathleen Hughes. Your patient nature calmed many storms during the writing of this book. Thank you!

And finally, to each of the fabulous, intelligent, and talented women who contributed to this book—endless thanks for sharing your lives so that other mothers and families might benefit.

Introduction

Why Is That Woman So Familiar?

I made it! 10 AM. It was standing room only as I leaned against the wall of the doctor's waiting room, and I began to reflect.

It had been an exhausting morning. All my time and energy had been devoted to feeding and dressing my three-month-old baby and two-year-old toddler so that I would be on time. My routine had focused on timing the baby's nursing schedule so that he wouldn't be hungry during my appointment.

Now, the doctor was running an hour behind, and the baby would soon be hungry again. I wondered nervously how I would nurse him in the crowded waiting room. I felt the sensation of a let-down in my breasts. What if wells of milk leaked? Could I discretely nurse him while standing against the wall? Would the elderly faint? Would teenagers stare? Would mothers cover their children's eyes?

"Mrs. Conners?"

Hallelujah! I gathered up the toys and the diaper bag, which felt as if it were filled with rocks, and lugged my uncooperative toddler and my baby in his heavy baby carrier into the examination room. But from there, the wait continued, and the stress mounted. My toddler immediately glommed onto a metal stool on wheels and began pushing it around the room, bumping it into medical equipment. He fell down. He cried. When I finally persuaded him to stop opening and closing the hazardous waste box, he discovered the stirrups. Clang! Clang! Clang!

Where was the doctor?!

My baby was awake now and beginning to cry, so I placed him on my breast as I continued to chase my toddler around the small enclosed area. Twenty minutes had passed since we had been ushered into the examination room.

Then I smelled it.

A poopy diaper.

I placed my baby back in the carrier. He began to cry again.

I sat on the floor and began to change my older son's diaper.

With a brief knock, the door swung open and I looked up.

She was beautiful and stylish with her form–fitting size 6 suit, hair perfectly tied back in a tight bun, and nails professionally painted to match her lipstick. She gracefully glided forward but was met by a powerful invisible force. I watched numbly as her entire body recoiled and her head snapped to one side.

I recognized the symptoms immediately. By simply opening the door she had detonated the stench in the once pressurized room. Only parents of very young children can pass through its blast without flinching.

Attempting to regain her composure, and being a tenacious woman, the doctor pushed herself through the barrier, as one might push through a wall of Jell-O.

With her face scrunched in disgust, she pointed her perfectly manicured finger at the reeking diaper. "We'll need to make special arrangements for that!"

I studied her. I had never met this woman before, but something about her was strangely familiar.

As I pushed my large bottom off the ground, I tried to compose myself. Glancing at my reflection in the mirror, I realized that wasn't going to happen, so I opted for a feeble smile.

"What brings you here?" she asked, practicing her shallow breathing technique in the foul-smelling room.

To my own amazement, I replied in toddler language, "I've had to go peepee a lot lately, and I think I might have a bladder infect ..."

"Perhaps you are pregnant," she said flatly.

"I don't think so, but if I am, you can go ahead and shoot me," I laughed weakly. I studied a large piece of dried mud on my right sneaker and glanced over at her shoes. My eyes were met by the blinding glare of her unscuffed Italian pumps.

"What type of birth control do you use?"

"Well, I just had a baby, and I've been breastfeeding, and ..."

"Breastfeeding is not a safe form of birth control," she announced.

"Yes, I know; but to be honest my husband and I can hardly even think about sex right now ..."

"We will proceed to do a pregnancy test; and if you're not pregnant, we will start you on birth control."

"I'd rather not take hormones while I'm breastfeeding; and, besides, the last time I tried an oral contraceptive it caused me to have some problems with depression ..."

"Was anything else occurring in your personal life that might have been the actual cause of that depression?"

The brief joust was over; that insult was the final lance. Her condescending words and tone had shattered my claim to being a mental health therapist and transformed me into a mental patient.

I attempted to defend the last vestige of my personal and professional integrity. "I have a master's degree in psychology. I was a therapist for almost eight years. I teach college psychology part time. Certainly I considered that possibility . . ."

She left the room before I could finish my sentence.

What had happened to me? I took inventory. I was completely exhausted. I smelled like sour breast milk. I was overweight. My enormous secondhand "transition" jeans were from Goodwill. My sweatshirt was stained with spit-up. My hair was a wiry mess. I hadn't had time to apply makeup that morning. I had lost my ability to think, and I was no longer able to hold a normal conversation.

Only two years earlier I had been a professional mental health counselor at NASA's Dryden Flight Research Center. After five years with the government, I had been promoted through nine grade ranks and had received several merit awards. While counseling, I also helped pioneer the creation of the NASA Dryden Child Development Center and initiated the Dryden recycling program, volunteered with the equal employment mediation program, and headed the dispensary's controlled-drug inventory. I had performed all these responsibilities while working on a master's degree program at night. Each of these tasks I had managed with professionalism and ease. Yet here I was, a complete physical and psychological wreck, and all I had to do was show up and survive a doctor's appointment.

She returned with a prescription for birth control and hustled me out the door. Suddenly I understood why she seemed so strangely familiar.

I used to be that woman!

CHAPTER 1

Stepping Out

Society is always taken by surprise at
any new example of common sense.

~ Ralph Waldo Emerson

The Illusion of Quality Child Care

*I*n the same way a young child might believe in Santa Claus or the Tooth Fairy, I believed in child care.

I once viewed child care as the magical answer to many of the problems plaguing our country's youth. I passionately believed only a decade ago that quality child care was far superior to the care provided by an "untrained" mother in the mentally unstimulating environment of her home. In fact, I believed in it so deeply that, while I was employed at the National Aeronautics and Space Administration (NASA) as an employee assistance program specialist, I joined a group of women who shared my opinion; and, together, we formed a committee to create the NASA Dryden Child Development Center. In a short time, I became president of the board.

Members of our board attended conferences, read books, and received professional consultation as we united to build our perfect center. There was little we didn't know about child care, and we applied our newly acquired knowledge to the creation of the best child care center in the country. We would accept nothing less than perfection.

Yet, soon after the center was finally operational, I began to question my beliefs about the benefits of child care. Although the facility met all the standards set forth by the National Association for the Education of Young Children, it was cold, sterile, and institution-like. The rooms were crowded, and I wondered how a child could compete against eleven others for a caregiver's attention. The teaching staff, high school graduates with only a few mandatory early education courses under their belt, struck me as immature and unqualified. Although I hesitated to voice my concerns, my core beliefs about the benefits of child care were changing quickly. Shame replaced the pride I had once felt in our new center, and I began to question whether I would place my own child in such an institution.

An Imperfect Transition

I left NASA in 1994 for a position as a mental health therapist with chronically mentally ill adults at a hospital in Bakersfield, California. This was soon followed by a counseling appointment with the state's Kern County Mental Health Children's Department. I also began to teach psychology at a local community college in the evenings.

In January 1996, I gave birth to my first child, James. Much to the surprise of my friends and husband, I left my career to become a stay-at-home mother. With a commute lasting over an hour each way, and my belief in child care shaken, it wasn't a tough decision for me to make. At the time, I didn't realize just how great a leap I had taken, but I was soon to find out.

Once home, I quickly realized that although my positive beliefs about child care had changed, my negative beliefs about stay-at-home mothers had not. I had assumed that my transition from career to at-home parent would be simple and quite beneath me. I confess I saw myself as overqualified for the position of mother and far superior to the average, uneducated, stay-at-home parent. But I quickly found the undertaking to be much more difficult than I had anticipated.

I was completely unprepared for my new role. On arriving in the previously uncharted territory called home, I took an inventory. I soon discovered that the only small kitchen appliance I owned was a coffeepot. I had planned to toss my baby on my back like Sacagawea and continue my journey; but, instead, I found I could barely hold onto the part-time teaching position I had opted to retain.

My life had been my work, and without it I found myself spending hours each day hanging out on the couch with my baby, watching daytime soaps to kill the festering boredom. Regardless of my ability to tackle enormous amounts of stress in my career quite masterfully, I became completely overwhelmed by and often tearful at the inconsolable cries of my colicky baby. As time passed, I found that I had little in common with my former colleagues at work. I had in fact become isolated at home. I swore I could actually hear my own brain cells imploding from atrophy when I tackled the monotonous and never ending tedium of household chores.

It wasn't long before I experienced the first phase of an identity crisis. While filling out the forms in the pediatrician's office, I debated over how to answer the question of my "employment." I wondered if it was fair to keep my old title, or if I would be seen as a burden to society if I used my new title: "homemaker." I often found myself envious of my husband's success at work and the simple freedoms he had, such as going to lunch with coworkers or traveling out of town. Although I truly believed that I had made the very best decision for our child, a part of me ached for the days when I was assured of my competence, knew who I was, and felt like a contributing member of society. My self-esteem disappeared with my previous identity, and depression filled the void.

Although it's now embarrassing to admit, I sometimes found myself fantasizing about meeting famous people and living an interesting and exotic life. A movie star owned property nearby, and I wondered if we might become friends. These thoughts, which seem so strange and foreign now, were part of what filled the chasm created by the loss of my career. The therapist still within me wondered if perhaps I wasn't starting to lose my mind. In some ways, I think I was.

Welcome to My Life

Before I continue, let me make a few confessions. I am not the perfect mother. Although I made an honorable attempt at becoming domesticated, I continue to fall short. For example, after many failed attempts at baking my children's birthday cakes, I now buy them at the grocery store. I've convinced myself that dust is a natural wood preservative and, therefore, refuse to polish the furniture until just before company is expected to arrive.

If you were to make a surprise visit to my home, you might experience the following scenario: You ring the doorbell and hear the muffled sound of a woman (me) hollering in the background, "Michael, get your shoes out of the living room!" As the door opens, you are greeted by a very embarrassed woman (me again) dressed in a T-shirt and jeans who begins a lengthy apology for the condition of the house as she reluctantly lets you in the door. ("She'd probably do well to apologize for the condition of her hair as well," you say to yourself.) You maneuver your way through the numerous toys on the living room floor and wait for her to remove a piece of gum from the couch as two boys, dressed in only their superhero underwear, streak by engaged in a medieval joust. Meanwhile, her angelic-looking daughter is painting her toenails, and the couch, with bright red polish. After determining that the gum removal project might take a while, you excuse yourself to the powder room (ignoring my cautions). As you pass the guestroom, you note an impressive, volcanic-shaped pile of unfolded laundry on the bed. After obsessively washing your hands to remove the invisible viruses you are certain you picked up from the doorknob, you return to the living room and attempt to enjoy some simple chitchat. It doesn't take long to realize that an actual conversation is not possible with the baby screaming. So, after removing the various toys the baby has added to your purse, you announce your premature departure. Walking toward your car, you glance into the minivan in the driveway and note a happy meal compost pile fermenting in the back seat and think, "Wow, what a great place to grow a vegetable garden!"

Reflections of Time

As a mother of four young children, I am speaking to you from the trenches. Life with small kids can often feel like an exercise in raw survival. I wish I could tell you how wonderful I am at it, but there are many times when I look just like other stressed-out, crotchety mothers, the kind you might see at the grocery hollering at their out-of-control kids.

And it is in such moments that I am occasionally tapped on the shoulder in a stalled checkout line. With food flying and small arms waving wildly about me, I listen in numb silence as a sweet, elderly voice of wisdom whispers, "You're going to remember these days as the best of your life."

Excuse me? The best days of my life? "How can she say that!" I wonder. "Can't she see I haven't slept in weeks? One of the kids has wiped snot on my shirt, and THIS one won't stop screaming! By the way, I'd like to know the name of the evil incarnate who decided to stack the candy next to the checkout line! Speaking of lines, why is every line moving except mine?! Who is this lady, and why is she telling me this? Is everyone on Prozac around here but me?"

You will no doubt someday experience a similar situation and respond in your own way. But I truly didn't understand what these strangers in the grocery line meant until I received the following letters from elder female relatives:

Dear Christine and Tim,

We received your Christmas greeting and the picture of your family. What a fine looking group! Michael reminds me of your father when he was a little one.

We aren't sending Christmas cards this year. Your Uncle Barney is not well. I'm so busy taking care of him, and it's about all I can do to find a meal for myself.

Hate to send a letter with such news this time of year, but thought I should tell you. Have a wonderful Christmas. Remember: These are the years you will treasure!

Love, Aunt Rebecca

The same Christmas, I received the following note from Germany:

Dear Christine, Tim, and Children—

Wishing you a wonderful season. It has snowed here and the garden is beautiful and very Christmas-like. It reminds me of

when my children would play in the snow. This past summer,
my husband passed away. It is still very lonely for me. My
arthritis is bothering me greatly. Enjoy your children while you
can.

Best wishes,

Your Omi

These letters serve as a powerful reminder that, although life with children can be difficult, we are likely to look back on this time as one of the richest stages of our lives.

Listening to Our Inner Voice

We've been given a strong instinct to love, protect, and be near our children—in a way, mothers possess a grizzly instinct. A parent, particularly a working mother, who leaves her child for hours each day must endure a mental struggle between the desire to protect and be near her child and the need or desire to work. The result is what the counseling world calls cognitive dissonance—a conflict between inner opposing thoughts. This conflict can often cause high levels of anxiety and inner turmoil. But, unlike a mama grizzly, we humans can repress these feelings by intellectualizing, denying, and rationalizing. Over time, we may learn to overcome this anxiety to the point where it is neatly repressed.

I recall a December 2000 *USA Weekend* article by a war correspondent who had just become a new mother. In the article she detailed how having a child dramatically changed her perceptions of mortality. Her child was only six months old when she was asked by her network to cover an outbreak of violence in Israel. She had already spent a decade on the front line in hot spots such as Somalia and Rwanda, and in her mind she had seen it all. But now, with the birth of her child, she had a different perspective. She was surprised to find herself fearful about leaving her child and the safety of her home and family.

I assumed that the correspondent would have decided to remain with her child. Instead, she talked herself into believing that her profession was more important than either her own safety or more noble than her role as a mother. She resumed her dangerous career.

She seemed to have it all backwards. The feeling she described is the natural anxiety a mother should feel when she is apart from her young child. This reaction is neither morbid nor irrational; it is quite normal and healthy. But in order for the correspondent to repress this anxiety and pursue her dangerous career, she had to view her maternal feelings as unreasonable and her position as a war correspondent as superior to that of a mother. This example typifies the feelings of many mothers. The more prestigious the career, the easier it is to make this justification.

This point is well illustrated by an event that occurred recently. I was attending a birthday party for a four-year-old friend of my daughter's. There was the usual array of parents watching their children and engaging in the standard party chitchat, but one woman looked confused and out of place. She approached me and asked who the birthday boy was. She apologized for her ignorance, stating that she was an optometrist from another city. "Usually my husband attends these events because he lives in this town. I'm only here on the weekends," she added.

"Oh," I said, "you're divorced?"

"No," she replied, "I have a private practice, four hours away, so I visit my family on weekends."

"Until you are able to move here?" I said, confident of her answer.

"No, I have no plans to move here. Because I'm in private practice, my clients need me. I have no one I can refer them to if I leave. It would be very hard for me to start another private practice in this town, so I must continue my work in the other city."

I looked at her son playing with the other kids and felt a wave of nausea.

How could a mother have more empathy for the needs of her patients than for those of her own child? Do her patients wait with childlike excitement for their appointments with her? Do they go to bed thinking of her? Do they cry when she leaves them?

Let's contrast the decisions of the war correspondent and the optometrist to those of two women who followed their grizzly instinct.

As Jenny writes:

> *When I had my first baby, I was still teaching. He was born in October, and I went back to work eight weeks later. My mom and my mother-in-law were watching him, which was wonderful, but I cried every day when I dropped him off. I thought, "They've already raised their kids, and now they get to raise mine!" It just didn't seem right. It never got better. I cried every morning. The next school year, I had my second baby. She was born in December. I was scheduled to return to work in February, but decided that I would not. My husband was a little unsure about this, but my mind was made up. I didn't go back! That was six years ago, and we have since had three more children. Believe me, it is work! But it is much more rewarding, much more fulfilling.*

Although Jenny may have tried to convince herself that leaving her children each day was okay, her heart never let go. Despite the fact that her children were in the care of their loving grandparents, she still grieved. Today, she is a mother of five children under the age of nine. Her stress is enormous, but her heart is at peace.

Donna tells a similar story:

When I was pregnant with my son, Ryan, I was employed as a design engineer. I worked until two weeks before my due date. I had no idea what motherhood would be like, but I planned to return to my job, at least part time, a few months after giving birth. My father had died when I was six years old, and my mother had to work to support my brother and sister and me. I had always been determined that I would be financially independent. I never wanted to be a housewife. I never wanted to depend on a man for the roof over my head. I wanted a career and a family, too. I had the career I had always wanted. The family idea was new to me, and I was pretty vague on the specifics.

Ryan was born a week early. He had some medical issues and was moved to Children's Hospital for surgery when he was only one day old. The surgeon corrected his problems, and his prognosis was good. Still, the sight of his tiny body strapped to a table with tubes and hoses everywhere was overwhelming. After four days, he was released from the hospital and sent home with us. I remember lying on my side on the floor in his room staring at him as he lay next to me. I couldn't get my fill of his contented little face.

I had been somewhat prepared for his arrival. The nursery was decorated and well stocked. I had read a few parenting books. We had most of the things he needed. What I was completely and utterly unprepared for was the way this tiny new person

had stolen my heart. I was in love with him, and he was
irresistible. The bottom line was that he needed me, and I
would have moved heaven, earth, and any part of hell for that
tiny little boy.

The Most Noble Profession?

Let's face it. Contemporary society has taught us that a career is noble and that staying home with children is an easy way out. It's not glamorous. It's not interesting. It's not lucrative. It's not necessary. It's really only for those less educated individuals who aren't successful in the career world.

For you who believe you are more important in your career than you are at home, I have news for you. You can be replaced in your career, but never as a parent. We can fire off a long list of the mistakes our parents made and their long-term effects on our lives; yet, when we consider our own role as parents, we somehow think our decisions won't have the same impact on our own children.

Perhaps you've spent years studying for your present position or working your way out of menial jobs, and now you fear the damage that a long absence might have on your career or financial situation. Maybe you take pride in the many awards you've received over the years or feel you would find life boring without your regular travel perks. Maybe a large part of your identity has been formed around the important people whom you call your friends and the respect you receive at social gatherings. The truth is, right now, it may be impossible for you to visualize yourself performing any role except in the career you love.

These fears are normal, considering the magnitude of the decision: when a mother steps away from her career to raise her children, she is making one of the greatest sacrifices of her life.

CHAPTER 2

The Changing Perceptions of Child Care

Children are the living messages we
send to a time we will not see.

~ John W. Whitehead,
The Stealing of America

The issue of child chare is extremely controversial. While quality care in moderation has been shown to benefit the cognitive and social development of some children, the truly heated arguments surround the definitions of "quality" and "moderation." What do these terms really mean when it comes to having your child cared for on a regular basis by others? Most parents agree that poor child care or excessive use of it would not be in the best interest of their young child. But what constitutes "poor" and "excessive?"

Sometimes, the answers are obvious. Show up unannounced at a short-staffed, non-credentialed child care facility, and you may see what I mean. Other answers are elusive and can only be found by truthfully considering your situation, searching your heart, observing your children's response to child care, or listening carefully to what they might be trying to tell you about their experiences there.

Some mothers must work outside the home. Many of these women wish they could be home, but circumstances prevent it. An acquaintance recently told me of a lawyer friend who left her career to be home, only to discover that her husband was having an affair. As the marriage dissolved, she had no choice but to return to work. Life is unpredictable, and the results are not always perfect.

I also have many friends who continued to work full-time when their children were young. These were wonderful mothers, and their children are happy and thriving. I can empathize with women who might be reluctant to leave the career they have worked so hard for. In fact, all it can take is a rough day at home with the kids for most of us to want to rush back to the sanctuaries of our careers. I understand this; and if the decision for a mother to leave her career was easy, I would not have written this book.

Let me make it clear that the purpose of this chapter is not to attack working mothers. But the truth is that pitfalls and dangers do abound in the caregiving business, and I have witnessed them firsthand. When a mother makes the decision to leave a career to be home with her child, her career is not all she leaves behind. Gone too are the stress, risks, and concerns associated with finding a safe child care arrangement that provides a loving, stimulating, and stable environment. This is no small blessing.

So it is for those of you who are contemplating leaving your careers, and for you who have already done so, that I've written this chapter. It is designed to validate and support your decision to be home with your children.

But all of this is a subplot to the fact that we are embarking on a major life event. Making a successful transition from career to home requires that we understand why we are doing this. If I thought that it made no difference to our children whether we held a full-time job outside the home, I would be the first to suggest we all return to our careers.

Surrogate Parenting

The relationship between a parent and child is unique, and it cannot easily be supplanted. But many mothers unknowingly attempt to do just that.

Davina, a banker, found the ideal nanny. The arrangement worked well until her son turned six, and she tried to wean him from the mother-surrogate he had known all his life. Not surprising, her son began acting out and showing excessive clinging behaviors toward Davina. Her warning, on the Web site, Tinies Childcare, is instructional:

> We all swallowed this stuff about how a child needs one consistent caregiver, but that it didn't have to be a parent. As long as the child had one key person, he would do well. The perfect nanny was our excuse to get on with our careers and believe we were doing the best for our children. But the primary caregiver being a nonparent only works if the parent is truly unavailable…dead, for instance. If the mother is flitting on and off the scene, as I was, the child doesn't understand why the mother is not fulfilling the role she plays in all his storybooks.
>
> Now I think we should worry less about finding the perfect nanny and more about making sure that we are central enough in our children's lives for the nanny not to matter so much. Do we want the perfect nanny for our children's sakes, or to let ourselves off the hook?

New Reports on the Problems with Child Care

Many experts argue that child care has no negative effects on children and can, in fact, actually promote a child's healthy social and cognitive development. Some proponents of child care postulate that, when a mother is fulfilled in her career, this positive energy is somehow passed to her children.

What follows is a quote from Davis and Palladino's textbook, *Psychology*, that I used not long ago for a class I taught:

> *In addition to contributing to children's cognitive and language development, placement in quality day care ensures that children receive appropriate inoculations and good nutrition. Good day care may also assist children's emotional development and help create better relationships between them and their parents. Day care provides some relief from the demands of parenting and can reduce stress because parents are assured that their children are receiving high-quality care.*

Just as urban legends and e-mail hoaxes have a way of lingering for years, so does the myth that child care is equal or even superior to a parent's care. Let's examine some of the latest research.

The Connection Between Behavioral Problems and Time in Child Care

From 1990 to 2000, a team of researchers supported by the National Institute of Child Health and Development (NICHD) conducted the most comprehensive child care study to date to determine how variations in child care affect children's development. Researchers followed 1,364 children from 10 different cities and tracked most of them through the first seven years of their lives. The study looked at children in various child care settings, including relatives, nannies, preschool programs, and large child care centers.

The NICHD study found that children who spent most of their time in child care were three times more likely to exhibit behavioral problems than were those cared for primarily by their mothers. Seventeen percent of the children who spent more than 30 hours per week in child care were regarded by teachers, mothers, and caregivers as being aggressive toward other children. This figure is compared to only 6 percent of the children who spent fewer than 10 hours per week in child care. Other behavioral characteristics noted included defiance and disobedience in kindergarten. These findings held true, regardless of the family's socioeconomic status, the sex of the child, or the quality of the care.

Children who spent more time in child care were also initially rated by the NICHD study as being more fearful and despondent than other children, although these specific differences seemed to disappear by kindergarten.

Study Links Working Mothers to Cognitive Impairment

In addition to increased aggressiveness, the same NICHD study stated that early maternal employment negatively affected some children's intellectual development. Lead author of the study, Dr. Jeanne Brooks-Gunn, summarized the NICHD findings in a July 17, 2002, article in the *New York Times*:

> What we found was that when mothers worked more than
> 30 hours (per week) by the time their children were 9 months
> old, those children, on average, did not do as well on school-
> readiness tests when they were 3 years old. In other work
> we've done, we've seen that those negative effects of early
> full-time maternal employment persist among children who
> are 7 or 8.

Three-year-olds from an average home environment, whose mothers did not work by the child's ninth month, tended to score at the 50th percentile on the Bracken School Readiness test. This test assesses a child's knowledge of colors, shapes, numbers, letters, and comparisons. Children of mothers who were employed by the ninth month had average scores at the 44th percentile. In addition, boys were shown to be more vulnerable than were girls to the effects of maternal employment.

According to researcher Jane Waldfogel, who was quoted in the same article: "That's a significant difference. I think moms and dads have to balance a lot of different considerations, but if it is at all possible for mom to stay home longer, or go back to work part time in the first year, that may be a good thing."

Child Care Associated with Increased Stress Hormone Levels in Children

In a 2003 study, the Institute of Child Development at the University of Minnesota found that children younger than age three had elevated levels of cortisol, a hormone associated with stress, after they spent a full day in day care. This hormone level fell after the children spent more time at home. Cortisol levels in the saliva of day care children were highest in those judged by caregivers to be the shyest. According to the study's lead author, Dr. Megan R. Gunnar, those elevated levels, although not sufficiently high to indicate signs of psychological trauma, are nonetheless cause for concern.

Today's proponents of child care can no longer argue successfully that child care is beneficial to a child's cognitive and social development. However, because these beliefs are so widely entrenched, a cultural paradigm shift is needed before this new research is recognized, validated, and accepted.

Which Factors Make Child Care Potentially Unhealthy?

Several factors unique to child care may explain why it can lead to increased behavioral problems, slower learning, and elevated cortisol levels.

Instability—Reliable and stable child care is difficult to obtain. As a result, a child often moves from caregiver to caregiver, forming and severing relationships each time. Most child care centers are actually structured in a manner that supports this process. Children, as they progress through the years, are *expected* to matriculate from one caregiver to another. Some programs matriculate all children at the end of the school year, while others advance children on their birthday. This practice may be logical in a child care setting, but not to a young child who is unable to understand why the caregiver is gone; and many internalize the loss.

Turnover—The very high turnover occurring in most child care centers only makes matters worse. In April 2001, the Center for the Child Care Workforce and the Institute of Industrial Relationships published the results of their joint study, "Then and Now: Changes in Child Care Staffing, 1994–2000." The study considered 2,000 child care centers during three separate periods: 1994, 1996, and 2000. The researchers selected only centers seeking accreditation by the National Association for the Education of Young Children (NAEYC) or rated "high" in quality based on the nationally recognized Early Childhood Environment Rating. The study found that between 1994 and 2000, 51 percent of the centers had a change in directors, and that in a *one-year period* between 1999 and 2000, the average rate of teacher turnover was 30 percent.

I observed the effects of high turnover on a child in my son's kindergarten class in a small private school. The child stood out among his classmates because of his regular troublemaking. He was frequently short-tempered, often sent to the office, and made little or no eye contact with adults. The parents, however, were seemingly kind and considerate. What then might have been the problem?

Mom and dad both worked; mom, in fact, had two additional part-time jobs. They had recently purchased a new home in a more desirable neighborhood, and the need for additional income became inevitable. In the year that we knew this boy, we watched him go through three different after-school child care arrangements.

Moreover, because the school was small, people noticed when the child's parents failed to attend kindergarten programs. While the other children enjoyed the attention from their proud parents in the audience—waving, winking, and snapping pictures—this little boy stood in the back with arms folded, refusing to sing, while the surrogate of the day attempted to show interest.

Children naturally bond with those who care for them. But child care is a business, and young children are incapable of understanding that they are a part of a business relationship. So, when their earliest bonds are repeatedly severed, as is often the case with child care, is it any wonder they suffer?

Reduction in Quality Time—A major problem associated with holding onto full-time careers is the lack of time available for parenting. Child care proponents have tried to advance the concept that *quality* is more important that *quantity* in terms of time spent with children, but the truth is that both quality and quantity are required.

A common misjudgment underlying the theory of "quality time" is that we can create it at will—as though we can simply walk through the door at the end of the day, and make it happen. It's not that simple. I learned this lesson firsthand in my relationship with my own father.

Because my parents were divorced and he had a new family, I rarely had the opportunity to be alone with him. So my well-intentioned stepmother would occasionally attempt to create quality time by saying, "Christine and David, why don't you go in the living room and spend some time together." I'm sure my father was as uncomfortable as I, because the suggestion generally resulted in the two of us sitting together in awkward silence.

A few years ago, I was lying in bed with our three oldest children. My son, James, was reading a story out loud about a girl who was learning tae kwon do. James, not familiar with this martial art at the time, pronounced it, "tae kwon doo." My middle son, Michael, suddenly sat up straight and announced, "*I know* how to spell doo-doo!"

"Really?" I replied, wondering if this interchange was something I should encourage.

"Yup! D-O-D-O!" He announced.

"No, baby, that spells 'dodo.' A 'dodo' is someone who can't spell doo doo."

For a moment there was silence—then roaring laughter. For more than a minute, my children and I giggled and laughed and giggled and laughed some more. It was a spontaneously joyous moment, unorchestrated, yet perfectly delightful.

Quality time is not something scheduled in your planner like a trip to the park. More often, quality time happens on its own terms. It might be a serious chat in the car on the way home from school, placing a Band-Aid on an invisible cut, helping your son with his first steps, or teaching your daughter how to read. The more time you spend with your children, the more opportunities you'll have for real quality time.

Quality of Caregivers—Every parent should be concerned about the quality of teachers at child care centers. Teacher salaries comprise the largest expense category in operating a child care facility. Most centers engage in a never ending struggle balancing tuition costs and offering teachers a reasonable salary. Because most parents are unwilling or unable to pay large sums for child care, it is the teachers and, ultimately, the children who lose. To put it in perspective, according to "2004 Current Data on the Salaries and Benefits of the U.S. Early Childhood Education Workforce," published by the Center for the Childcare Workforce, the average child care worker in 2003 earned approximately $17,000 per year.

Low wages have been cited as the primary cause of high caregiver turnover; but low wages also imply that most child care centers do not have the option of hiring the highest-quality teachers. Findings from a 2001 study, entitled "Then and Now: Changes in Child Care Staffing, 1994-2000," reported that new teachers were significantly less educated than the teachers they were replacing and were less likely to live in households that met the self-sufficiency standards for their communities. During the 1990s, welfare reform also contributed to a sizeable population of former welfare recipients entering the day care profession. The study determined that, by 1998, 35 percent of the centers in the study employed individuals who formerly received welfare. Again, recall that these centers were selected for the study based on their desire to meet NAEYC accreditation standards and for their reputations for quality care.

All parents require occasional child care, and I am no exception. Several years ago, following our move to Cincinnati, I spent considerable time investigating the part-time and drop-in options in my area. One morning, I visited a nearby center where the director only reluctantly agreed to show me the facility. In one classroom, a young preschooler sat crying in the corner, apparently in time-out. Suddenly, a large man appeared and removed the child. I froze with fear. *Who was he, and where was he taking her?*

I was told later that he was the janitor. Would any parent feel comfortable with the janitor having the authority to remove a child from a classroom?

This center was one of the many that call themselves "educational" and give their caregivers titles such as "teacher." A question for parents: When we look beyond the titles, do we really know who is responsible for our children?

The Russian Roulette of Child Care: What You *Don't* See Is Often What You Get

According to the U.S. Census Bureau, more than 17 percent of the nation's children are cared for by nonrelatives, either in their own home or in the home of the nonrelative provider. The problem with home care by nonrelatives is that it lacks oversight. Because young children are often unable to relate the events of the day, some parents have installed hidden cameras in their homes. The increase in the use of "nanny cams" has also led to a dramatic increase in the rate of nannies losing their jobs. According to CNN.com, "It is estimated that 70 percent of all [nannies] lose their jobs because of what parents see on videotape."

Judith Lederman, a former public relations executive and author of *Searching for Mary Poppins: One Family's Quest for Perfect Child Care,* hired and fired over 25 caregivers before she finally left her six-figure job to stay home with her three children. Lederman relates hair-raising accounts of her many attempts to find the perfect caregiver. She says, "For the most part, I found neglect."

Some parents might breathe a sigh of relief that Lederman discovered *only* neglect and not abuse. But what is neglect if not a less obvious form of abuse? And what exactly are we paying caregivers for if not to watch over and protect our children? But neglect *is* common, and I have witnessed it firsthand. Because I had an occasional need for part-time care, a friend recommended a nearby in-home day care that accepted drop-ins—a service not easy to find.

On the surface, the provider appeared capable. She watched children during the day and attended childhood education classes at night. Her goal was eventually to operate her own day care center. Sounded ideal. Unfortunately, I discovered that it wasn't.

I used her services infrequently, but I grew increasingly uncomfortable at what I was witnessing. Because I dropped my children off at atypical times during the day, I observed events that other parents might have missed. For instance, I saw the TV on constantly, a baby who always seemed to remain in his car seat, junk food served for lunch, and a house that often became so cluttered I grew concerned for the safety of the babies. Despite the fact that the caregiver had almost completed her bachelor's degree in early childhood development, no lessons or programs were offered that might enrich the children under her care.

One morning, I went to the door and knocked. No answer. I glanced through the window by the door and saw that the caregiver appeared to be sleeping on the couch. When I knocked again, she opened her eyes and came to the door. We both pretended as if nothing happened. I convinced myself she was resting, nothing more. Soon after, the same situation occurred. However, this time she was sound asleep and did not wake up after repeated knocks. I watched for a while as toddlers, barely able to walk, waddled around the room handing small toys to babies in car seats, sharing bottles, and basically taking care of themselves. I returned home. The caregiver called me later that day.

Sitter: Where were you? Weren't you going to drop off Maria?

Me: I tried to, but you were asleep.

Sitter: I was just resting my eyes. You should have come in.

Me: I knocked several times, but you didn't wake up.

Sitter: Oh. [Pause] So are you going to drop her by?

I didn't. And I never went back. A short time later, I learned that other parents had simultaneously taken their babies out of her care as well.

Michelle, a veterinarian, had this experience:

Initially, I put my daughters in a day care that was right next door to my office so I could visit them during my lunch break. I frequently found my girls in very wet, soiled diapers. They often would have a bad case of diaper rash after a day spent at the day care. I would see the workers pick up pacifiers off the floor and put them back in the children's mouths. The children who did not complain as much were left in cribs and swings for what I considered an unacceptable amount of time. Many mothers would bring their children in with fevers, diarrhea, and vomiting, exposing all the other children to whatever they had. At this day care facility, my first daughter developed chronic ear infections that eventually left her eardrums scarred. If the day care hadn't been next door to me, I would have removed them quickly.

After taking my children from this facility, I hired a nanny, which worked out well for us. The nanny's name was Tina, and she ended up being with our family for five years. During that time, Tina had to leave us for a few months; and I hired a young college girl to replace her. After she watched them the first time, my girls, though they were young, begged me to not let her come back. I listened. Several months later I learned that she had HIV/AIDS, and I ended up needing to have my girls tested.

Sometimes children are physically abused. According to ABCnews. com, Jennifer and Brett were first-time parents who thought they had done everything right when they hired Claudia to take care of their baby. They found Claudia through a professional agency, checked her references, and hired a private investigator to run a background check. An apparent bite mark on their five-month-old child's face, combined with crying and squirming when she was handed over to Claudia, led them to review their home videotapes. What they saw horrified them. One scene showed Claudia raising the baby over her head and slamming her on the floor over and over again. In another scene, she shook the baby back and forth so hard that her head snapped back. The frequently forgotten lesson of this story comes to us from the baby's father, "A stranger with glowing recommendations is still a stranger."

Becky, a mother of four, recalls her own child care nightmare: "When I was a child, the four teenage grandsons of my babysitter repeatedly raped me." An even more horrific aspect of Becky's story is that after her mother, a bank manager, found out about the rapes, she continued to let the same woman care for her daughter. Becky's firsthand abuse was the primary reason she left her career as a teacher to stay home with her own children.

Several years ago, a friend contacted me regarding the daughter of a mutual acquaintance. The girl was exhibiting unusual sexual behaviors, and her mother, who worked full time, was naturally concerned. Because most children at some point display interest in their sexuality, it isn't always clear whether a particular behavior is out of the ordinary. But this case appeared odd. For example, the child was compulsively rubbing her private parts against the couch while moaning. I suggested that the mother investigate whether the girl might have been abused while in child care.

Several weeks later, I learned that, unbeknownst to the mother, the drug-using, unemployed son of the babysitter had moved back home. For weeks, the mother had been dropping her daughter at the babysitter's house unaware that her babysitter's son was also at home all day. The mother immediately removed her daughter from that situation.

Another mother tells a similar story:

> I only needed child care on an occasional basis. A friend recommended a woman she knew, and so I felt pretty comfortable with the arrangement. One day, I stopped by to pick up my daughter. I knocked on the door and a wave of fear swept over me. When no one opened the door, I panicked. I let myself in. To my right, my babysitter sat facing her husband on the couch. Neither looked at me when I walked in the room. No hello—nothing. I looked down and found my baby daughter naked and spread-eagle facing my babysitter's husband. At first glance, it looked as if they could be changing a diaper, but they weren't moving. "What's going on?" I asked, really starting to freak. My babysitter attempted to try to put the diaper on my baby, but, for some reason, she couldn't. I grabbed my daughter and ran out the door. The babysitter called me later and apologized. She claimed to have taken a heavy painkiller that had made her very drowsy. I don't know what really happened that day; it makes me sick to think about it.

Care by Grandparents

Twenty-one percent of American children receiving child care are cared for by their grandparents, a proportion that continues to grow. This solution may appear to be perfect: we personally know the providers, they genuinely love our children, and the cost of their services is usually low. According to Census Bureau analyst Kristin Smith at www.census.gov, however, "Only 15 percent of grandparents were paid for taking care of their preschool-age grandchildren, with payments averaging $40 per week. Day-care centers received twice that amount, averaging $83 per week."

In situations where parents may have difficulty caring for their own children, such as in cases of divorce, drug or child abuse, or parental death, grandparents often must assist or risk losing their grandchildren altogether. In such crisis cases, grandparents can be an enormous blessing.

In other situations, grandparents may be torn between the pride they have in their child's career and their concern for the well-being of their grandchildren. To prevent their grandchildren from being placed in the arms of a stranger, they step in to fill the parenting gap.

On the surface, grandparents serving as regular caregivers may look like the perfect child care solution. Unfortunately, this arrangement also has problems.

The well-being of the grandparents must also be taken into consideration. New studies, found at www.parentingtoolbox.com, report that excessive caregiving may be unhealthy for grandparents, particularly when they must also assume the full-time role of parent. Ron Huxley, a licensed marriage and family therapist, shares his observations:

> Grandparents feel grief due to the fact that, just when they
> are ready to retire and enjoy the finer things of life, they are
> faced with the responsibilities of caring for their grandchildren.
> Many grandparents feel they have failed as parents due to
> the fact that their own children are unable or unwilling to care
> for their own children. And grandparents, like single parents,
> may have fewer resources, both emotionally and physically,
> to go through the act of re-parenting. Not only are they older
> and have less energy to take care of the needs of the children,

but they are also given less financial compensation and legal power to make decisions.

The 2001 study, "Physical and Mental Health Status of American Grandparents Providing Child Care to Their Grandchildren," confirmed Huxley's observations: extensive care for a grandchild was associated with elevated levels of depression, with one in five grandparents who provided extensive caregiving having clinically significant levels of depression.

As with many things in life, what might be wonderful in moderation becomes a problem in excess.

No Regular Care

It is astounding that the 1997 Census found that 37 percent of parents requiring child care claimed to have no regular child care arrangement. I was acquainted once with a couple who operated this way. They both worked independently, she as an in-home nurse and her husband in construction. Each morning they would awaken, not knowing who would be watching their children that day. So each morning, a new crisis unfolded that would inevitably result in a heated argument, followed by desperate calls to friends and family to see who could watch their children. In our last conversation, my friend revealed that her then 10-year-old daughter had developed panic attacks and preferred to stay at a friend's house rather than return to her chaotic home.

Assessing Risk

Viewing the act of parenting from the perspective of risk assessment can be helpful in understanding and controlling the problems that child care often introduces. Mothers and fathers instinctively scan for the innumerable hazards that threaten their children's well-being. Without knowing it, parents continuously weigh risks to determine if they can be ignored or whether they demand intervention and management. Proper parental risk assessment leads to informed and wise decisions that protect and nurture our children.

We use risk assessment in selecting a car seat or choosing the type of food for our baby. It is especially appropriate to extend the process to assessing child care. Potential hazards lurk behind the decision to use child care and the duration and type of care selected.

All mothers, even those of us who don't work full-time outside the home, require the services of child care providers. Doctor appointments, lunch with friends, dates with spouses, education or volunteer activities, even part-time work—these events and many others require some form of assistance. (It is with some irony—dare I say guilt?—that I have to confess to using child care, although *limited*, just to meet the draft deadline for this book!)

However, when we ignore the risks associated with child care, or fail to properly assess them, our analysis becomes flawed. We have potentially placed the well-being of our children at stake. By letting career goals and ambitions cloud our judgment, by being unwilling to sacrifice unnecessary personal objectives and material things for the good of our children, we gamble with their health and happiness.

CHAPTER 3

The Transition Adjustment

*We must become the change we want to
see in the world.*

~Mohandas Gandhi

To work or not to work; that question provides fertile ground for some of the most heated parenting debates of our time. By simply conceiving, a woman is soon thrust into the middle of a bitter battle of opinions between moms who work outside the home and those who choose to stay at home. Nor are the battle's participants necessarily limited to mothers: the rest of the world seems to have chosen sides as well!

Once pregnant, you will have nine months to make your decision and learn all of the negative connotations associated with your choice. The opinions from the opposing sides boil down to this: you can be a selfish, child-neglecting career mother, or you can throw away your education and waste your life on the couch, eating bonbons and watching soap operas. No matter what your final decision is, there will always be someone who thinks you made the wrong choice. Either way, you can be sure that guilt will follow.

The essence of this feud is revealed in the first rejection letter I received as I was marketing the idea for this book. It came from the editor-in-chief of a small publisher.

Hi Christine,

I'm a working mother of a happy, healthy 2-year-old. As such, I'd have a hard time publishing anything that claimed: "Today, no parent can ignore the numerous studies that demonstrate

the negative consequences of child care on a child's emotional
and intellectual development."

You might consider allowing that there is no study that shows
definitively that one or the other method (stay-at-home vs.
working) is "better" than the other. I think your book could still
be a worthwhile and amusing addition to the parenting shelf,
but I would encourage you not to polarize your audience.

Best of luck with this elsewhere,
Ann

After discussing the contents of this letter with several people, some
of them suggested that I eliminate the first two chapters of this book, which
clearly "polarized my audience." They told me that this type of material really
had no place in a self-help book, and that it would be almost impossible
for me to find a publisher if I left it in. The two chapters, after all, were only
background material and not the focus of the work.

For quite some time, I contemplated this advice, stung by the
rejection, yet not wanting to ignore what I held to be true.

Know Why You Are Home

After avoiding my computer for several months, I was having a
particularly bad week. It began with my husband leaving on a business trip
to Europe. I was stuck at home with a new baby, his three young siblings,
seven baseball games, three karate classes, two dance lessons, and one violin
recital. On top of it all, one of my sons came down with a virus; I stepped on
a shard of glass that I wasn't able to remove from my foot; and, of course, I
started my period.

One evening, in the middle of this very challenging week, I came
home from a baseball game to discover that a cat had pooped on my front

porch. I immediately used the water hose to jettison the unwelcome pile out into the darkness of night. Or so I thought.

The next day, a neighbor came to the door. I noticed his face was tight and puckered and that he purposely seemed to avoid eye contact. After his premature retreat, I stepped onto my porch and was horrified to discover that, in the darkness of the previous evening, I hadn't actually sprayed the cat's present from the porch, but had only moved it to cover the step below. Now, in broad daylight, it glistened proudly for all to see.

Later that evening, I returned home from baseball pictures and the violin recital with all four kids in tow. The week had been grueling, so to bring some happiness to the chaos, I purchased three jelly donuts for my children, which I had left on the kitchen table for their return. What we discovered was a scene that could have come from *The Twilight Zone*. When we had left home earlier in the day, there were three donuts. When we came home, there were two. Where did the missing jelly donut go? Who ate it? An intruder must have helped himself while he pillaged the house in our absence! I nervously searched all the rooms and closets, but all seemed to be in order.

It wasn't until later the next morning, while I was limping through my living room (the glass shard still stuck in my foot), that I solved the unnerving mystery. There, on the white carpet behind a lounge chair, was a half-eaten donut, keeping company with a mound of colorful jelly donut cat puke. Yeah, I know, real cats don't eat jelly donuts.

Overwhelmed by my repulsive discovery, I left the florescent red treat to lie on the carpet and stain it. Instead, I chose to cut the grass. It was while mowing my little square of weed-infested suburbia, defeated and near tears, that I contemplated returning to work.

I fantasized what it would be like to be in an air-conditioned office, wearing a spit-up-free outfit, discussing cerebral matters over lunch with coworkers, my purse full of extra spending money, a shiny boat in my back yard; but, most important, someone else at home cleaning up the jelly donut cat puke.

But just when I was about to host the biggest pity party in town, I recalled the information I shared with you in chapters one and two. Like a slap to the head, I remembered that I wasn't home for my sake, I was at home for the sake of my kids. I can't tell you exactly how many times I've had to remind myself of this simple truth in the 10 years since the birth of my first child, but trust me, it's a large number.

So I've retained the first two chapters. Because, whether you're in the midst of wrestling with the enormous decision to leave your career or just having a very bad week after you've decided to do so, you occasionally need to be reminded, like I do, just why it is that you are home.

This Ain't No Vacation

Some people will see your new job at home as a vacation from your real career, but the reality is that you are about to embark on one of the most challenging, demanding, stressful, and, yes, at times, more painfully mundane jobs you will ever encounter. For those of us who have spent most of our lives trying to achieve our own self-directed goals and dreams, this can be a rude awakening.

Dr. Brenda Hunter, psychologist and author of *Home by Choice: Raising Emotionally Secure Children in an Insecure World*, exemplifies the extent of the challenge. Even though the purpose of her book is to encourage women to stay home with their children, she herself was unable to do so. In her own words, she felt "lonely, depressed and empty. I ran from my deepest self—I went back to work."

In reality, few of us anticipate the psychological difficulties we may encounter when we embark on the often-humbling lifestyle of a stay-at-home parent. The virtual absence of self-help materials on the subject only serves to make our struggle with this adjustment appear somewhat irrational and petty. "Am I the only one going through this?" we may wonder. "How is it that I can hang out in bunny slippers all day long and yet find life so difficult?"

I spent a great deal of time analyzing my own transition and the rather dysfunctional adjustment that I made to it. As I spoke to other stay-at-home parents, I realized that I was not alone. Although most at-home parents believed they had made the right decision, many still experienced career-to-home adjustment problems at some point.

The Diagnostic and Statistical Manual of Mental Disorders, Fourth Edition (DSM-IV) applies the diagnosis of adjustment disorder to those individuals who experience symptoms such as depression and anxiety for at least three months after a stressor has occurred. The manual lists numerous stressors that can cause adjustment disorders. These include leaving the parental home, marriage, becoming a parent, failing to attain occupational goals, retirement, embarking on a new job, divorce, a physical move, financial difficulties, life-threatening illness, disability, and the death of a loved one.

It is curious that the therapeutic world has not given serious attention to the transition from career to home, which can include several variations of these events. Yet, consider the many changes that can take place during this transition:

- BECOMING A PARENT
- LOSING A CAREER

- FAILING TO ATTAIN OCCUPATIONAL GOALS

- REDUCTION IN DAILY ADULT CONTACT

- ONSET OF MIDLIFE ISSUES

- SUDDEN LOSS OF INCOME

- LOSS OF TANGIBLE GOALS, PURPOSE, AND IDENTITY

- LACK OF SENSE OF ACCOMPLISHMENT

- LOSS OF INDEPENDENCE

- REBALANCING OF POWER IN THE MARRIAGE

- CHANGES TO PHYSICAL APPEARANCE, USUALLY RESULTING FROM PREGNANCY

Not all parents have difficulty adjusting. Some are able to tie on the apron, grab the diapers, and get to work with a smile. For these individuals, many books are available with helpful tips on everything from making homemade play dough to planning the perfect birthday party. But others will struggle with the transition and may encounter problems such as depression, stress, anger, anxiety, parenting difficulties, loss of identity, fluctuations in self-esteem, and marital issues.

To have problems adjusting is not a sign of character weakness or mental illness. Adjustment problems are a normal psychological response to a major life event. It is important to appreciate that leaving a career initiates a chain of events that can, indeed, be classified collectively as a major life event.

Grieving the Loss of Career: The Five Stages of the Career-to-Home Adjustment

Dr. Elisabeth Kübler-Ross, a Swiss-born psychiatrist, identified five stages that patients pass through when they learn they are dying. These stages have also been applied to other life losses such as ending a relationship, losing a limb, aging, and job burnout. They can also be applied to the career-to-home adjustment.

Denial—Denial is a psychological defense mechanism that serves to keep us from dealing with reality. I recently had an encounter with denial when I asked a friend if she would allow me to interview her for this book. She replied in a somewhat hostile tone, "Well, I am not a stay-at-home mom, I am a business consultant!"

I said, "But you did leave your career and now work part-time out of your home, correct?"

"Well, yes, but I can assure you that I am very busy!"

For some, even the idea that they might be associated with a group of women who have, over the years, been stereotyped as ignorant, lazy, and boring is enough to firmly plant them in denial.

Anger and Resentment—This stage is hard to miss, and the anger associated with it can come from several sources. Examples are the endless boredom of chores and the resentment that you, and not your spouse, had to forfeit a career. Our marriage can become the dumping ground for this anger.

Bargaining—After you've left your career, you may find that you are constantly debating whether to return to work, how to work, or when to work. You may be forever attempting to invent unique ways to work part time. If so, you may be trapped in the bargaining stage. This is particularly likely if your last conversation with the boss regarding your decision to leave sounded something like this:

> Jerry, it won't be long. I'll be back soon; I'm doing it for the baby, you know. So if you could hold my job for me, that would be great. Oh, you can't? Yes, I know it's been three years since I left, but I am planning on coming back soon. I think I made that clear. You gave Mary my office? Wow, THAT is heavy. Okay,

*well, I'm going to call you again in a few months and check in.
We'll talk some more about when I'm going to return to work,
okay?*

Personally, I've been bargaining in some form for over 10 years now.

Depression—Depression is good in the sense that it indicates that
reality has finally kicked in, and you are beginning to grieve over the loss of
your career. You miss your coworkers, the income, the status, the clothes,
and the action. As you settle into your new life, you finally realize that
cleaning products don't bring joy and elation as advertised.

Acceptance—Acceptance is the final stage, and the goal, of a
healthy transition. With acceptance, you have established a new identity,
the characteristics of which I discuss in the next chapter. Your self-esteem
blossoms, and you are at peace with your decision. When you come to the
place where you no longer feel the need to tell every stranger on the street
what you used to do for a living, you have reached the stage of acceptance.
You know who you are, not simply as your job title defined you, but as the
whole of your existence defines you.

Very few people pass through each stage in an orderly fashion. Most
of us bounce back and forth between them. If you are like me, you might
work through all stages and return later to repeat one or more of them.
Take heart, though. This is a normal experience.

You Are Not Alone

When you first step into your bunny slippers, you may feel very
much alone. Many of the other parents with whom you are acquainted are
more than likely the ones you met at your former place of employment,
giving you the biased perspective that all career mothers return to work
quickly after giving birth. But there are others out there just like you,

educated, intelligent, and talented, who are also setting aside their own dreams temporarily for the common good of their family. And while it might appear old-fashioned to do so, when we consider the current research, this altruistic act is becoming more in vogue.

Beginning in the 1970s, American culture saw a sharp rise in the number of mothers who worked outside the home. According to the Bureau of Labor statistics, in 1975, 39 percent of mothers with children under age six worked outside the home. Today, that proportion is 62 percent.

Many of us viewed this cultural progression from the windows of our day care center as we waved goodbye to our exhausted mothers each morning. Unfortunately, there also was a sharp increase in another important societal benchmark during this same period. According to the U.S. Census Bureau, the number of divorced individuals more than quadrupled, from 4.3 million in 1970 to 18.3 million in 1996.

Today, we have the benefit of hindsight. While we certainly appreciate the advances made in women's rights, we now also see how important we are in our roles as mothers and wives. Despite the sharp increase in women working outside of the home during the period since 1975, the latest census reveals a reversing trend: the percentage of women who returned to work within one year after giving birth dropped from 59 percent in 1998 to 55 percent in 2000.

Are women tossing aside their education and careers for a 1950s' version of motherhood? Of course not. Instead, it appears that mothers are recognizing that life is not just one large monolithic event, but rather a collection of seasons, many of which change rapidly. Women are beginning to understand that, as they accept and adjust to each new season for what it is, they are better able to experience it more fully. The substitution of bunny slippers for high heels is only temporary. The season passes, but the rewards persist—and they are considerable.

CHAPTER 4

Your New Identity

Bloom where you are planted!

- Mary Engelbreit

Our Career Identity

When you have a career, your identity is clear, your title is respected, and your life purpose is unquestioned. Your clothing, car, and home speak of your identity, and the title on your badge validates your mission. So what happens to our identity when we step away from our career?

Actress Brooke Shields shared her own struggle with this question in an interview in the May 2005 issue of *Good Housekeeping*:

> *One day, I decided to take Rowan to the studio lot to visit friends from the crew of* Suddenly Susan. *I knew they'd be thrilled to meet my little girl. It was such a familiar environment that I felt like I had returned home. As we reminisced about how much fun we'd had, I started to get weepy. People kept commenting on how great it must be for me to be a mom and to not have to deal with the craziness of show business. It seemed to me that in their eyes, I was no longer an actress. Yet I felt that I wasn't handling my current "job" as a mom so well either. My sense of identity was shaken.*

Ms. Shields's career identity may have indeed been shaken, but it was not lost. Despite how she may have felt at that moment, she did not lose her talents as an actress simply because she was taking time off for her baby. Instead she became an actress at home with her baby. If you were an engineer, and you decided to join the Peace Corps to plow fields for a couple of years, you would be an engineer plowing fields. You are no less an engineer because you are plowing fields, any more than you'd be less of an engineer if you were mowing your grass on a Saturday.

What you have earned is yours to keep, whether you are currently employed in that capacity or not. If and when you decide to return to your career, your education and experience remain an important part of your total identity. So, if someone asks you what you do for a living, there is nothing wrong with mentioning your career history with your current status as a stay-at-home mom. Be clear, this is not the same as denial. Denial comes from a place of insecurity. Denial is to be embarrassed that you are at home. Never be embarrassed that you are home.

Our Home Identity

To our career identity, we add our "at-home" identity. Unfortunately, the names given to mothers at home aren't particularly impressive. "Housewife," despite its current use in popular TV shows, is rarely used nowadays in normal conversation. Most stay-at-home mothers despise the term because it conjures up images of June Cleaver, feather dusters, and the smell of Pine-Sol®. "Homemaker" is hardly better, but at least you can smell the chocolate chip cookies. The term, "stay-at-home mom," only tells us where the mom is located. It doesn't say much beyond that.

These titles are part of our identity problem. Some sociologists believe that labels can instill personality traits. They argue that when a criminal is given a label associated with a past crime, for example, he is likely to internalize this label, so he is more likely to commit similar crimes in the future. This theory has also been applied to parenting. When we discipline a child, we teach parents to say, "That was a bad thing that you did" as opposed to, "You are bad." When we use the latter, we give the child a label. If he embraces this label, it becomes a part of his identity, and he is more likely to go on to do other "bad" things.

When we adopt a label like "housewife," with all of its negative connotations and images, it's like putting on an oversized, shapeless dress. It just hangs over us, hiding all of the wonderful curves and revealing little of the creative and successful person beneath. What's worse, our own negative biases against housewives are likely to send us into an unconscious attack against ourselves. If you had secretly judged stay-at-home mothers to be lazy, unsuccessful, and boring, you will likely see yourself as all of these, too.

Some have tried to transform the negative images of stay-at-home parents by giving them such fancy titles as "domestic engineer" or "CEO." In my opinion, the work of a stay-at-home mom is not a "career," and the efforts to make it so sound as silly as calling SpongeBob SquarePants a "hamburger design technician." Let's face it. The efforts to upgrade our status with fancy titles and job descriptors have done little to change society's image of the stay-at-home mom.

Recently, a friend recalled an appellation she once heard as an American child growing up in Nicaragua in the 1970s: *alma de casa,* or "soul of the household." This is a unique twist on the more common designation, *ama de casa,* or "housewife." I asked a physician acquaintance, originally from South America, for her comments on the use of this title. This was her reply:

> *It makes sense that women should be called* alma de casa
> *since they are amazing multitasking beings. Women are the*

ones who take care of the house, the health of the children, the husband, the economy of the household, reproduction, and they are responsible for transmitting wisdom and knowledge from one generation to another.

So, here it is, soul of the household, a designation women can take pride in, one that captures both the spirit and the purpose of our venture. We haven't sacrificed our career aspirations to have a personal relationship with our home or to bake chocolate chip cookies. We are home because we recognize that there is a deep calling to motherhood, and we have chosen this life path over power, success, independence, money, and status. We have chosen to be the alma de casa.

Your Identity Style

Many new almas, unfamiliar with the world of the stay-at-home mom, attempt to become the stereotypical supermother. They launch themselves into their interpretation of this role, cooking, baking, and sewing with great fervor. Some believe that if they do them well, these activities will bring as much fulfillment to their lives as their careers once did. In reality, many seek domestic bliss, only to find the role empty and incompatible with their personality.

Kim, a physician, describes her own attempt at this role:

Initially, the idea was that I was going to be home to be with my child, and that was it. But somewhere in there, I started to get the idea that I had to be supermom. I would take over all the household chores and duties since I was now home, and perhaps also be a crafty, sewing mother with a green thumb. I discovered quickly that I was not good at it and did not want to be all those other things, and I went back to the idea of first and foremost spending time with my child and asking for help

*with some of the chores. I forgot about the other stuff that I
had originally thought moms at home were supposed to do.*

You may be pleased to know that you don't have to be a supermom
to qualify for the job of stay-at-home mother. The styles of almas vary, just as
the styles of career women do. Here are a few examples:

Island Mama—The attitude of the Island Mama is laid-back and
relaxed. Whether she's at home or at the mall, her clothing is as casual as
her attitude. Being a practical woman, she recognizes that at some point in
the day she will be awarded the white badge of courage (spit-up), so she
dresses appropriately for the occasion, unconcerned about what others
might think of her carefree attire. Impressive statistical fact: Island Mama's
children are responsible for almost all of the marshmallow cereal consumed
annually.

Earth Mother—Earth Mother takes a natural approach to
parenting. Earth Mother delivers her babies without medical intervention,
breastfeeds them until they are too heavy to sit in her lap, and lets them
sleep in the family bed until they become teenagers. She is acutely aware of
the impact her child has on the environment, so she refuses to let her baby
wear anything but cloth diapers. She makes her own organic baby food and
only gives her children whole grain cereals. She has established a recycling
center next to the changing table, and she celebrates her child's birthday
with cakes made from organic soy powder and carob frosting.

The Educator—The Educator sees her primary mission as the
intellectual and cultural advancement of her children. Each poster on her
child's wall has been clinically proven to raise her child's intelligence quotient
by five points. The background music is always classical, with Baby Einstein,
foreign language tapes, and daily public radio commentary interjected
occasionally. Her planner is filled with special events at the library, concerts,

and various exhibits at the science and art museum, and she tests her children for Mensa before they enter kindergarten.

Mountain Mama—Mountain Mama drives a big truck, not because it's cool for chicks to drive trucks, but because she needs it to bring home felled firewood and lost hikers. She prefers the outdoor activities with her children to the ones indoors. She is a mighty arm-wrestling opponent and will take on any bear that messes with her vegetable garden or her children.

Society Mum—Society Mum identifies herself by what her husband does, the home she lives in, the car she drives, and the brand-name clothes she and her children wear. She places her children in the most expensive schools, not because they are actually the best, but because they are notoriously the most expensive. She is keenly aware of what the other high society mums are wearing and doing and strives to emulate them, creating what appears to be a breed of cloned housewives with similar hobbies, cars, hairstyles, and plastic surgery. You can recognize the high society mum whether she's dropping off her kids at school or running to the grocery, because her hair and dress are eternally impeccable. Her child's birthday parties are catered and always include a large farm animal.

Your style might be one of the above, a combination thereof, or none of those listed. Whatever the case, as you venture into this new world, consider your style and be who you are. You have already proven that you are a talented and creative woman. Instead of trying to emulate the styles or stereotypes of the supermom or any of the other moms around you, fearlessly define your own style. Be a super mom if that's you; but if it isn't, don't be afraid just to be yourself. The career-to-home adjustment can be an incredible time of self-discovery, but only when you are true to yourself.

Social Identity

Don't be surprised if you find yourself feeling a bit out of sorts socially. Your niche, after all, was in the career world. You understood the career mentality, the shared goals, the drive to succeed, and the satisfaction of a job well done. But as time passes, you may discover that you don't fit the career profile anymore. It may become increasingly difficult for you to relate to your former coworkers and they to you. You may, in fact, have become something else entirely. A stay-at-home mother? You don't exactly fit this mold either. It's as if you are floating somewhere in between two social identities, unclear exactly where or how to fit in or where you'll land. Jenny, a special education teacher and mother of five, discovered this the hard way: "I was discussing my children when an old friend from work said, 'You really shouldn't talk about your children so much; it's boring.'"

In an attempt to connect with other mothers at home, I made it a habit to avoid discussing my career. Lest I appear proud, I limited my conversations to safe, universal topics such as children, marriage, and the horrors of housework. I realize now that the unfortunate result of this irrational concern was that I missed a lot of the interesting facets of the women I thought I knew.

Wendy was a person I thought I knew. She was my children's soccer coach for two years. Mother of four, I knew her as a likeable, down-to-earth person. One day, I saw her at the gym, and I mentioned this book. She listened with interest, then responded, "Yeah, well I had a career."

"Really?" I said, "What did you do?"

"I was a lawyer," she replied flatly.

I hollered with laughter. My kid's soccer coach was secretly a lawyer! I only wish I had inquired earlier. Suddenly, this woman, whom I had already found so likeable, had become even more interesting to me. What a shame to realize that, in the two years I'd known Wendy, the scope of our conversations only got as deep as the secret ingredient in her famous potato salad.

As I continued to seek contributors for this book, I was amazed to discover how many women around me had careers before coming home. Doctors, teachers, artists, and business managers, all disguised as stay-at-home mothers, living in my neighborhood, working out at the gym, taking their kids to story time at the library, and, yes, even shopping at the thrift store.

But the truth is this: You won't know who they are unless you ask. As Michelle, a veterinarian pointed out, "When we aren't in our work clothes, we all look the same!" So we must ask, "What did you do before you became a stay-at-home mom?" It's a question that rarely offends and may reveal many interesting facets about your acquaintances. Maybe that woman sitting at the other table at McDonald's camped out in a tree for a month to protect a forest from loggers, chased a famous rock band for a year, or biked across Europe. You'll never know how interesting the other stay-at-home moms are unless you ask.

Why seek these women out? The primary reason is to find other almas with whom we share a bond, a connection with someone who understands the loss and conflict involved in staying home the way we do. As a rule, those still possessing a career generally don't find your stories from the home front particularly interesting, and it is also true that many people at home aren't particularly interested in your career experiences. Almas, being hybrids, are more likely to find both your business plan and your stories of your child's projectile vomit equally fascinating. You may even consider starting a group specifically for almas. But don't just sit around and commiserate. Use your unique talents to do something interesting and worthwhile.

The purpose of finding other almas is not to segregate yourself from other stay-at-home mothers. Women who haven't had a career before motherhood often are at peace with what they do, and we can learn from this gift. It may also help to remember that just because a mother hasn't had a career doesn't mean she won't someday. Some women have children before pursuing their education or career goals. The fantastic doctor who delivered my daughter began by raising her children and then going on to medical school. I have no doubt that the time she spent at home is responsible for the unique empathy she has for her patients. People don't always take life in the same order we do, nor should they have to.

Establishing Your New Identity

The notorious problem with careers is that they can become all-consuming. Most careers necessitate specialization and require that we devote an enormous amount of time and energy to mastering our profession. It is in this process, over the course of many years, that we leave behind many of the facets that at one time made up our total identity.

As an example, when I was in high school, my total identity included many different hobbies, such as tennis, art, poetry, choir, cross country, flute, and surfing. I wasn't particularly skilled in any of these areas, but my identity was stable because it was a composite of several interests, not just one. If any of these pieces failed, there was no identity crisis because it was only one piece, of many.

When I entered college, it became necessary to specialize. For the next thirteen years, I spent the majority of my time studying and working in psychology. When I stepped out to become an alma, my career was the only component of my identity that remained. In fact, I was so consumed by my career that I failed to notice that it had actually hijacked my identity.

Barbara Kline, author of *White House Nannies*, offers an interesting perspective on this phenomenon. In an article by Ann Gerhard of the *Washington Post*, Ms. Kline describes the type of clients she serves. Perhaps you may recognize a piece of yourself in this article.

> *They call her suburban agency and start off by describing how important and busy they are. "By the way, Barbara, I run an empire," says one. Or they have the chief of staff call: "I represent a very prominent family." Eventually, after listing all their titles and every advanced degree, they toss in a phrase or two describing their children: "eight-year-old brilliant twins, a four-year-old gymnast, and a brand-new baby girl who can already sing on key."*

I can still relate to these parents and their emphasis on success. But I realize now that my career had become a crutch. When this crutch was removed, my identity fell apart. But just as adversity can inspire growth, it is also true that when we remove the crutch, we eventually learn to walk without it. If we don't allow ourselves the time it takes to learn to walk again, but instead drag ourselves back to the crutch of our careers, we inhibit the growth we could have experienced had we attempted to face this challenge.

Not long ago, I ran across my friend Doris at the park. It had been almost six months since she had left her career as a high-level government official, and she openly admitted that she was suffering from adjustment problems, in particular, depression. To escape these problems, she was desperately trying to return to her career. She explained: "Work and peers have always been more important to me than my immediate family. This pattern was established early in life. I have not had strong connections to my parents or siblings since early childhood. I've come to realize that my career is my anchor."

A career can indeed be an anchor that keeps our lives seemingly grounded and defines our place in the tumultuous ocean of life. But the problem with anchors is that they also hold us tightly in the same position, preventing us from growing. With an anchor, we can develop a false sense of security. If a tsunami were to approach our boat, as might happen if we were laid off or when we eventually must retire, this anchor would keep us from rising above the wave. Our anchor could ultimately become our demise.

Setting Sail for a New Identity

Let's imagine what might happen if you were to lift your anchor from its deep hold on your career. Your new freedom might give you a sense of instability, confusion, or fear as you drift from your place of safety into the expanse of an unfamiliar sea. You can sense the sharks butting your boat, representing the seemingly endless negative external and even internal messages regarding your decision. Large waves head your way, and, from a distance, you recognize these as depression, anxiety, and fear.

But you don't allow your boat to drift indefinitely. Instead, you start your engine, and, while it warms, you pull out your map and begin to chart your next course. You see that your map shows four islands, and you understand instinctively that each one has an essential component of what you will need to recreate your identity successfully. You point your boat in the direction of the first island, move the throttle to maximum power, and feel a wonderful sense of exhilaration as your craft leaps forward. As if by magic, your small boat has become a sleek, new yacht, designed for speed and agility. From your captain's chair you now hardly notice the sharks swimming below, and you are aware that even the waves appear smaller as your boat easily cuts through each like a hot knife through butter. You are on your way!

Isle of the Spirit—As your ship approaches the Isle of the Spirit, you immediately experience a calm serenity. This is the place where you will find your inner peace and rest. This island will help you learn to stay on course through churning seas and discover your life's greater purpose. Colleen, a chemist and mother of three children, shares her experience: "When I first came home, I had to learn to rely on God more than ever. Before I stayed home, I felt I was in control of my life and finances. After I left [my job], I felt like I had no control over anything."

While on the island, you establish a plan for meeting your spiritual needs and then return to the boat to continue your adventure.

Isle of Nurturing—As your boat approaches this second island, you see children, your children, the ones you already have and those yet to be born, playing happily on the shore. It is on this island that you discover your value and identity as a mother, the person who will be one of the most important and influential in your children's lives. Kim, a physician, shares her insights: "My philosophy has been to 'be in the moment' as much as possible. So I tried as much as I could to just enjoy my baby, and to be present as much as I could through his babyhood and toddlerhood without worrying about what others thought of my choice, or when or how I would go back to work."

Call to your children on the shore and welcome them warmly to this special season of your life.

Isle of Scattered Shells—As you approach the shore of the third island, you see that it is covered with beautiful shells, each representing a part of yourself that was left behind so you could concentrate on your career. Your old passions, hobbies, forgotten elements of your identity, these all lay before you.

Examine the shells from your past and carefully choose the ones you think will fit nicely into your new life.

Isle of Discovery—Nearing this final island, your attention is directed to a large wooden easel on the shore. Perched on the easel is a blank art canvas. It is on this canvas that you will paint the next stage of your life.

While the Isle of Scattered Shells was a place to rediscover yourself, the Isle of Discovery is the place where you uncover what you don't know about yourself. Maybe it's an invention or a business idea, a leisure pursuit, or an intellectual challenge. Rhonda, an accountant, found her creative outlet in her own home:

> Upon returning to home life, I have discovered that I have a definite creative side. I find myself taking time to arrange flowers, create outdoor gardens, scrapbooking my children's memories, and generally making my home a more beautiful place to live. I have the desire to create beauty and comfort in the environment where my family lives. Working full time as an accountant, and being a full-time military wife—with my husband serving in Iraq—left little time for the beautification of our home. If the beds got made and dinner was cooked, it was a major accomplishment. Today, I find that I have time to create wonderful meals and make my home a showplace. The greatest part is that I find I can do it all myself. I have learned to be a carpenter, painter, and handyman. I can design or fix just about anything, and my children love to participate. So I find them developing a creative side as well. Martha Stewart has nothing on me now!

Since it's impossible to know what the future will hold, you only need to take this canvas along with you. It symbolizes a commitment to stay open-minded and willing to explore the uncharted areas of your identity.

Each of these islands represents a unique part of the formula you will need to recreate your identity. But there are potential inhibitors to the process of which you need to be aware.

Impediments to Recreating Our Identity

There are five common inhibitors to recreating our identities: fear, anger, substance abuse, career-centric thinking, and television (yes, television).

Fear—Fear is an obvious inhibitor to growth, but most fears are never realized. We spend an enormous amount of time concerned about things that do not come to pass. For example, time and again, people tell me they would like to write books, yet few of them ever do. Why? They fear rejection. Yet, most published authors have been rejected, not once, but many times. The biographies of all successful people contain examples of numerous failures.

Challenge your fears and don't let irrational thinking dictate the next phase of your life.

Anger—All too often, people use anger as an excuse to stay stuck. They blame others for the condition of their lives in an effort to disguise their own failures. If you have a long history of blaming others for the limitations in your life, it might be worthwhile to examine your anger in therapy.

Substance Abuse—Substance abuse is notorious for inhibiting personal growth and stunting maturity. When we abuse drugs and alcohol, we temporarily escape those issues that need to be dealt with while creating a list of additional problems in the process. Instead of growth and maturity, we end up with regression and immaturity.

Career-Centric Thinking—Career-centric thinking leads to judging the value of life's efforts according to the narrow measurements of achievement, status, and money. Many of us were raised to be career-centric thinkers and even chose our line of work according to this often shallow set of parameters.

Don't allow career-centric thinking to keep you from enjoying the activities that will bring you the most joy. Use this unique time at home to learn to liberate yourself from the expectations of the rest of the world.

Television—For the typical person, there is nothing more time-consuming and unproductive as watching television. According to tvturnoff.org, the average American spends more than four hours per day in front of the television set. That amounts to approximately 120 hours each month learning little and accomplishing nothing.

I've been asked on numerous occasions how it is that Tim and I accomplish so much with so little time. The answer is simple: we don't watch much TV. Although we occasionally view a DVD, we avoid the temptation to become a remote control zombie by not subscribing to cable or satellite programming.

You've been given only a short time on this earth to accomplish great things. Why waste it in front of the TV?

Tying It All Together

Let's tie all the pieces together.

I am an alma, therapist, and author. Because of the number and ages of my children, most of my life is spent on or near the Isle of Nurturing. Every day, I expend an enormous amount of time, energy, and money to assure that my young children and husband have a stable home environment where they can be nurtured and feel safe, find regular meals, have clean clothes and a reasonably tidy home, get help with their homework, and be chauffeured around town as needed.

My visit to the Isle of Discovery resulted in something I would have never imagined. When I became an alma, I had no idea that I would someday write backpacking cookbooks with my husband. To this day, Tim and I still laugh about what a strange detour that was. But what began as a mutual hobby has now become an important part of both of our identities.

The books began as a creative outlet spawned by the location of our former home in California. The Pacific Crest National Scenic Trail, which runs from Mexico to Canada, passed near our home, and we often hosted long-distance backpackers for a night or two to give them a break from the grueling life along the trail. We made it a hobby to collect backcountry recipes from our guests, and these eventually became the foundation of our first two books: *Lipsmackin' Backpackin'* and *Lipsmackin' Vegetarian Backpackin'*. Publishing these two cookbooks contributed to my ability to find a publisher for the work you are reading and has led to yet another contract for a cookbook for scouts.

If I were to judge our cookbooks strictly from a "career-centric" perspective, I would have to view these works as a failure. While they have performed very well for their genre, I am definitely not Steven King and have yet to make the *New York Times* Bestseller list. I could never make a living from what I have published. Despite this, Tim and I will always view the process of writing and publishing these books as one of the more interesting experiences in our life.

I have also received hundreds of manuscript rejections in the 10 years that I've been home. But I have not let the fear of failure inhibit me. On the contrary, I have been able to experience great freedom in writing because the income from our book sales has never been relied upon to feed our family.

The shell I chose from the Isle of Scattered Shells was art. Today, I am pursuing a master's degree at the Savannah College of Art and Design. Financial and schedule constraints do not permit me to attend full-time. It may take more than a decade before I graduate, but it is no longer the degree that matters most. It is the joy of learning that I truly value. Unlike the classes I once devoured like a famished animal, today I take classes the way one might enjoy a fine chocolate. What I learn from each class is far more important to me than those arbitrary annoyances called "grades" and "degrees."

A fellow student recently suggested that I leave my husband so that I might become eligible for financial assistance. She reasoned that this would help assure that I might complete my degree in a more timely manner. Unfortunately, she was serious. This is an example of how dangerously narcissistic this world of achievement has become. Being well-acquainted with the Isle of the Spirit, comments such of these do not throw me off track or cause me to dream of a better life at the expense of my family. Because I remain spiritually grounded and have a strong commitment to my family, such harmful suggestions only strengthen my resolve.

If we return to my friend Doris, who once described her career as an anchor, we see that she wasted no time charting a new course for her life. Not content to sit idle, she launched an environmental consulting business from her home. The business allows her to continue the profession that she loves but also spend more time with her three-year-old son. Some might say she's discovered a way to enjoy the best of both worlds.

Pace Yourself

In leaving your career, you have been given an opportunity to recreate your identity. But this doesn't mean you should blindly fill every minute of the day and forget the reason why you are home. If overachievement is one of your characteristics, you may need to actively resist the temptation to dive into a renewed frenzy of activity. Work to establish a pace appropriate for the ages of your children and the needs of your family. And don't forget that your family is an important part of your healthy new identity.

CHAPTER 5

Saving Your Self-Esteem

> *No one can make you feel inferior*
> *without your consent.*
>
> *– Eleanor Roosevelt*

Our identity defines who we are, but it is our self-esteem that tells us how we feel about ourselves. In a sense, it is a measure of our level of confidence. Our identity adjusts slowly to major life changes, while our self-esteem rises and falls much more rapidly with the normal ups and downs of any given day. A surgeon, for example, might have high self-esteem if she has had an unbroken string of successful surgeries. But on the day she loses her first patient, her confidence will likely plummet, if only temporarily.

Healthy self-esteem is essential to the job of an alma. When our self-esteem is high, we enjoy more satisfying relationships and rely less on others to reflect our self-worth. When our self-worth is low, we may become dependent on others to feel good. This dependency can result in neurotic game playing and manipulative behavior. When we place the responsibility for our self-worth on our spouse, the result is a dysfunctional marriage. When we apply this same expectation to our children, we may ultimately damage their psyches.

Becoming an alma can certainly be a challenge to our self-esteem, but it doesn't need to damage it. By becoming aware of factors that affect self-worth, you can take a proactive role in raising your self-esteem during the challenging time following the departure from your career.

Self-Esteem Busters

Let's begin by taking a look at where some of the attacks on our self-worth originate.

Unsolicited Advice—The workplace can be an excellent place to find positive, uplifting messages. The daily challenges you tackle at work are intrinsically rewarding. Coworkers seek your advice, value your expertise, and compliment your work. Promotions, raises, training, and travel—all of these contribute to a sunny perception of yourself.

The home does not have these advantages. As a new alma you may be stunned to discover how much criticism you can receive in your new "occupation." Dr. Deborah G. Alicen described this phenomenon in her article in *Selfhelp Magazine,* "Navigating Motherhood."

> Mothers are open to criticism by almost anyone, at any time: from the child's father, from her own parents, from in-laws, doctors, nurses, teachers, friends, neighbors, day care workers, even passers-by on the street or in the supermarket—and, indeed, their children themselves, for not buying them that box of Crispy Crunchies when they are in the supermarket. And few, if any, of the critics take into account the very real and individual limits placed on each mother's time, energy, and resources—both internal and external. Nor do they generally take into account that a mother's job changes every day, along with the development of her child.

I probably have received more parenting advice from complete strangers than I've offered in a clinical setting during my entire professional career. Since most of it has been either obvious or useless, I have come to believe that unsolicited advice is typically nothing more than a subtle form of one-upmanship. The real message is: "You obviously don't have a clue what you're doing, but I can help."

As I began to write this chapter, I decided to document the unsolicited advice that I received over the course of one week. Here's how it went:

Monday—In my race to get my four children and myself to the gym in time for my aerobics class, I'd forgotten to put shoes on David, my baby. It wasn't a big deal; the day was warm and sunny, and he usually took them off when he arrived at the nursery anyway. But not everyone shared my laissez-faire attitude. As I was leaving the gym, a staff member stopped me in the hall to explain the importance of shoes. It was actually a nice lecture, short and sweet, but the underlying message was, "What kind of idiot forgets to put shoes on her baby?"

Tuesday—My baby was carrying his bottle as we entered the department store. I couldn't find a clean sippy cup as I ran out the door, so I grabbed the bottle. A greeter stopped me on my way in and began instructing me on the proper method of transitioning a baby to a sippy cup. It was a nice lecture, short and sweet, but the message was, "Clearly, you should know better than to let your child drink from a bottle at his age."

Wednesday—I mentioned to a friend that my son had discovered how to pull the tabs off of his diaper and was enjoying the pleasures of streaking through the house. She informed me that this was the sign that he was ready to potty train. She began instructing me on how one does this, seemingly oblivious to the fact that I had successfully managed to train his three older siblings. It was actually a nice lecture, short and sweet, but the message was, "Look. It doesn't matter how many kids you have, you still don't know what you're doing."

Saturday—I was grocery shopping when my baby started into a rather dramatic temper tantrum—following a script that he had recently perfected. I knew he was safely strapped in the shopping cart, so in an attempt to extinguish his inappropriate behavior, I ignored him. Instead, I focused on selecting a brand of cereal that my daughter and I both could agree on. From out of nowhere, a woman screeched, "He's going to throw himself right out of there!" I looked up, saw that my son was safe, and went back to debating fiber verses marshmallow content with Maria.

The woman apparently didn't appreciate being ignored, so she positioned herself between my baby and me, pointed an accusing finger at my toddler, and spit, "HE'S NOT WEARING A SEAT BELT, *IS HE?!*" I wish I could tell you that I politely replied, "Yes, ma'am, he is. But, regardless, I don't know how my son could have survived another day without wonderful people like you taking the time to look after neglectful parents like me. Thank you." But, instead, I stood up and faced the concerned individual. Other customers had also gathered to witness the scene of apparent gross neglect. In a loud and sarcastic voice, I inquired, "What is your problem?"

By now, my son had stopped his own fit to watch his mother begin hers. The aisle fell silent; embarrassed shoppers began to shuffle away. The woman stood there in disbelief. She had been so confident of my bad motherliness that she simply couldn't believe my son was actually buckled in. She tugged at the belt. Locked. Clearly disappointed, she mumbled something to herself and walked away. It was not a nice lecture, nor was it sweet, but the message was similar, "YOU are a *bad* mother!"

Nothing can be done about unsolicited advice other than to accept that it happens to all mothers. It may help to realize that most unsolicited advice from strangers is nothing more than inconsequential trivia.

If we examine the advice I described above, we see how little value it usually is. Sure it's good to wear shoes, but my child wasn't harmed by not wearing them. And who is the final expert on when a child should transition to a cup? Or the precise day that a child should be potty trained? Even true experts disagree about issues like these. Seeing as most adults eventually drink from cups and don't wear diapers, I figure the window for training my children is probably fairly large. And my son's strange behavior when strapped into a grocery cart? It lasted about one month, then disappeared.

Kelly, author and mother of one, shares her tried and true solution to busybodies:

> Late in my pregnancy, it was too uncomfortable for me to exercise on land, so I went to the community college pool. One day, I was standing on the deck with my huge belly, and some pinch-faced lady looked disapprovingly at me and asked nastily, "Does your doctor know what you are doing?"
>
> I looked at her and said, "I AM a doctor!" then jumped in, cannon balling a big tidal wave of water all over the deck.
>
> When people offer advice about an apparent medical issue that's none of their business, just tell them that you're a doctor, and they'll shut right up!

(Don't worry. Other than having a strong aversion to pinch-faced women, her son suffered no trauma from the cannonball incident.)

Mother versus Mother—The sport of hitting on your self-esteem isn't confined to strangers; people you know sometimes join the opposing team as well. I once received a call from a neighbor regarding my daughter:

> "There's something I've been meaning to speak to you about for some time. Something that concerns me."

"Yes?" I replied.

"Well, every time your daughter is at our house to play, she asks for food."

As a therapist, it seemed likely to me that my neighbor had conditioned my daughter to ask for food. "Well, have you been feeding her?" I asked.

"Just Goldfish," she replied.

Ah, Goldfish. Not a food product you're likely to find in most health food stores.

"Well, just stop feeding her the Goldfish, and tell her that she shouldn't ask for food," I said. Mystery solved. Or so I thought.

"Yes, I can do that; but I was concerned."

"About what?"

"Well, I was worried that she might be…[pause] hungry."

Wow! Did she think I was starving my daughter? It was a concept so far out there that I hadn't seen it coming. Could my neighbor actually have believed I might purposely deprive my child of food? Probably not, but sometimes this type of pseudoconcern belies a subconscious effort to establish oneself as superior at child rearing. In effect, this behavior is a form of insecurity, of which all parents are occasionally guilty. To the parent who is under the microscope, however, it comes across sounding like, "Hi! Just calling to remind you that I'm the better parent! Have a super day!"

I continue to work on my own spontaneous need to offer *my* opinions to other mothers, both friends and strangers. This may result, in part, from being a therapist and having a somewhat arrogant belief that everyone desires my valued expertise. Therapist or not, I have to remind myself that, unless another mother specifically asks for advice, I may actually damage her confidence by offering an unsolicited opinion that comes across as being critical.

Of course, there are times when criticism from other mothers is legitimate and justified. Legitimate criticism generally comes from those who know us best, whose intentions are genuinely good, and who want to help us, not hurt us. These are the times when we need to take a personal inventory and honestly face our own weaknesses. If our ego is healthy, we can own up to our mistakes, learn from them, and move on. Owning up to mistakes often necessitates including those made by our children as well (and, trust me, there are sure to be a lot of these).

In the case of my six-year-old daughter, although she certainly was not starving, I found that she did have a racket going in the neighborhood. She had discovered that, by using her Southern charm, she could coerce my neighbors out of their ice cream, candy, and, yes, Goldfish. The scam went like this: she'd show up at their door looking quite faint. While brushing imaginary sweat off her brow, she'd say something like, "I am sooo hot and hungry. Do you have any treats?" I had witnessed this form of drama at home on many occasions, but I was beyond embarrassed to discover that she had been using the same ploy with our neighbors.

Loss of Status—Author Tom Wolfe was recently quoted in the *Savannah Morning News* as saying, "The greatest motivating force in life, after procreation, is concern over one's status." Now whether you agree with Wolfe's statement or not, to some extent we have to acknowledge that, for many people, status can, indeed, be a very strong motivating force.

In the workplace, we have a clear understanding of our status. We know how we rank among our coworkers and understand what needs to be done to improve our status if we so choose. But what is this enigma we call status?

Some time back, one of my children was enrolled in a high-quality, part-time preschool program. Because of its location and reputation, I wasn't surprised that many of the women who brought their children to this school fit the category of "Society Mum." During drop-off and pick-up periods, the school's hallway looked like the runway at a designer fashion show. Women glided past each other in the latest styles, arriving for their final pose at their child's classroom.

It didn't take me long to realize that I didn't fit in. For one thing, I found the concept of getting all decked out to drop my child off at preschool a little creepy. Not only did I not get dressed up, my displaced "Mountain Mama" style was clearly working against me. I was snubbed.

But at this same school, I met a beautiful Hispanic mother who didn't fit the mold, either. Perhaps recognizing that we were both outcasts, she invited me out for coffee. We discussed the peculiar phenomenon of widespread snobbery at our children's school, and the conversation eventually turned to our careers.

My jaw dropped when she told me that she was a pediatrician. Not only was she an alma, but she was also an exceptional doctor, with credentials too many to mention. Before we parted ways, she made a comment that I will always remember. "Isn't it odd," she said, "that we are both accomplished women; yet many women think themselves so superior that they can't even return a simple smile?"

It had been easy for me to internalize the snobbery I had experienced as a reflection of some sort of failing on my part. Perhaps I could dress better, lose a few extra pounds, or walk a little more gracefully.

Yet, here I was having coffee with one of the most interesting mothers at the center, and even she was being snubbed.

Status is the quest for the intangible, a mere reflection of how we compare to others, nothing more. It is an outward grasping for an inner significance. When we place my doctor friend in a group of other doctors, we see that she is well respected and admired. Yet, when we place this same woman among a particular group of women, we find her snubbed and rejected. Has anything changed about her? No. She remains the same woman. The only thing that has changed is her environment. Status, therefore, is only a *perception* of one's significance.

I recently ran across an old black-and-white photograph from the 1920s of a dozen bathing beauties posing for a contest on the beach. I studied the picture for some time. In their faces I saw my friends, my neighbors, and, even myself. I caught glimpses into each of their personalities: playful teasing, controlled nervousness, outward annoyance, peacock pride, and hidden pain. It was a rare look at beautiful women as they were meant to be, without silicone breasts, tucked bellies, and sucked thighs. I reflected on the lives of these women. What were their dreams? Did they strive to place themselves among the rich and famous of their day? Did they feel envy when their neighbors bought a new Ford Model T?

Who today can recall, less than a century later, the status of these women? They have all probably passed away, and the contemporaries against whom these women might have ranked themselves are more than likely gone as well. Did anyone who lived during this period leave Earth with anything more than the others?

Michelle, a veterinarian who left her career to be at home with her children, applied this perspective to a recent experience:

As a veterinarian, I have to maintain a certain amount of continuing education every year in order to keep my license current. In the past, whenever I would RSVP for a continuing education event in the area, I was recognized. However, this time, when I called on behalf of both myself and my husband (who is also a veterinarian, but still works), I was told, "Yes, we know Dr. LeCompte (my husband), but who is Michelle Vallee (my professional name)? Is she a veterinarian or a layperson?" At first, I was speechless. It was like a slap in the face. Just a layperson? I wanted to say, "How dare you?" But then I got hold of myself and simply said, "No, she isn't a layperson. Michelle is a veterinarian, too." And I quietly put down the receiver.

It was a very poignant moment for me. After working all my life toward the goal of becoming a veterinarian, working as a veterinarian, developing client relationships, pouring my heart and soul into patients—after only a year and a half, I was quickly forgotten! As I thought about this, I realized that, as a veterinarian, my influence was limited. But as a mom, my influence was much deeper. I reasoned that this influence would be negative if I chose to devote all my time to veterinary medicine and little to my family, or it could be positive if I chose to devote my heart to my children and husband.

On tombstones, you never see words such as, "She was a beloved veterinarian, doctor, businesswoman, insurance salesman," and so on. By the end of our lives, we often finally understand what's important. I hope my tombstone will read, "Michelle—Beloved Wife, Mother, Daughter, and Friend," because of the time I've chosen to invest in people rather than a career.

To allow something as arbitrary and intangible as status to dictate our self-worth is a mistake. Referring to Tom Wolfe's quote, I enthusiastically suggest that we focus our energies on procreation instead!

Perfectionism—In many careers, perfection is not only a desired characteristic, it is an essential goal, if not an outright requirement. If a pharmacist makes a mistake in preparing a prescription, the result could be death. Many professions share the same standards. From engineering to health sciences, standards must be met or the results could be devastating. Most of us are in the habit of striving for perfection in our work, but when we apply that same standard of perfection at home, we set ourselves up for failure.

Consider the typical day in the life of an alma. The baby's diaper is changed, but he immediately soils it again. Minutes after you mop the kitchen floor, an open cup of juice tumbles to the floor. When you try to read a book to your baby, he rips the pages. Despite your attempts to maintain a pleasant appearance, you always seem to be covered in crusty food pieces. No matter how many parenting books you've studied, your children still behave like Neanderthals in public. The task of parenting can feel a lot like making sand castles at the edge of the shore: we rebuild over and over, only to watch our castles wash out to sea.

But the goal of parenting is not perfection, it's progress. While progress may seem invisible in the course of a typical day, that doesn't mean it isn't measurable or that it didn't occur. Progress begins at conception with the healthy choices you make during pregnancy, and it continues from there: with each push that brought your baby into the world, with your baby's first smile, first steps and words, and the first day at kindergarten. Progress is made with each story you read, each meal you serve, and each bandage you apply.

To measure progress, we can't look at the sink full of dirty dishes or the laundry piled to the ceiling. To appreciate our progress, we must look back to see how far we've come. We need to recognize that some day we will lament, "They've grown so fast!" Then, the full measure of the progress that has occurred in such a seemingly short period will become fully evident as our grown children leave home for lives of their own.

Guilt Trips—You would think that after sacrificing our careers, we should be entitled to live a relatively guilt-free existence. No such luck. Without knowing it, we simply have chosen "stay-at-home guilt" over "career guilt." Here are some of my favorite self-induced alma guilt trips:

Welfare Mom—Make sure to feel guilty now that you must leach off your husband financially. How dare you have it so good? While other women must do *real* work, you, on the other hand, get to stay home, watching soaps and eating bonbons.

College Bum—Don't forget about your parents, who nearly killed themselves to raise you to be a somebody. What do you do to show your appreciation? You waste your education so that you can stay home to watch soaps and eat bonbons.

Slum Lord—If you weren't so busy watching soaps and eating bonbons, your house would be cleaner.

Roseanne—Is it my imagination, or did Roseanne Barr give you an *Extreme Makeover*? Maybe if you weren't so busy eating bonbons and watching soaps, you'd have your teeth brushed by noon. Eeeuuw.

Child Neglecter—Since you have nothing better to do than eat bonbons and watch soaps, do you think you might be able to give your child the attention he needs? How dare you do the dishes during his prime waking hours? Have you read an armful of books to him today? Can he speak a second language yet? The other kids in day care can.

Bad Wife—If you were a real woman, you wouldn't burn dinner and turn your husband's underwear pink. In fact, you'd be able to give your husband the loving he needs *while* watching soaps and eating bonbons!

Me Guilt—Many of us experience tremendous guilt when we attempt to claim a little time for ourselves. We see the world of parenting as either black or white. Either you're at home dedicating every breathing minute to your children, or you're an evil working mother. There is no in between. This means that on those occasions that you do contemplate part-time work, a new hobby, downtime with your spouse or friends, a trip to the spa, or a college class, instead of enjoying this time, you find yourself burdened with guilt.

If you don't happen to feel naturally shamefaced, there's always some guilt peddler out there happy to help. Debra, a hygienist, received the following e-mail from a friend after she mentioned her desire to go back to school part time:

Debra,

It's really none of my business, but when my kids were young and my husband was working late nights, I felt that I needed to be home with the kids, and that my time would come when they were all eventually in school. It's just that your husband, John, looks pretty ragged these days. I remember Danny looking like that because of all the hours he worked, and I just tried to make the home life as easy as possible on him. Enough of my opinion.

Love,

Cheryl

Was Cheryl right? I say Cheryl should have minded her own business. Debra was a mother of three, and her youngest child was two years old at the time. Debra had been a full-time alma for six years, and, although she wasn't ready to put her youngest in child care, she openly admitted she was beginning to feel a little antsy. Her desired program required only two classes a week in the evenings, when her husband would be home. She was confident she could complete her homework assignments during her toddler's naptime, and her husband John was supportive of her plan. In fact, John viewed her time away as a positive factor, because it provided a structured routine for him to become more actively involved with their children. These classes were a part of the family's master plan. They hoped the course work would allow Debra to work from home some day, ultimately taking some of the financial burden off John.

All families are different, and what might be suitable for one may not work for another. The number of hours your husband spends at work, the amount of time he travels, the number of children you share, these are some of the issues that must be considered. The needs of each mother differ. One might be satisfied taking time off a few hours each week for a little tennis, while another may desire to work part time.

In a March 2005 article in *Elle* magazine, Judith Warner, author of *Perfect Madness*, gave us all something to think about:

> We're consumed with doing for our children in mind and soul
> and body, and the result is that we're depleted; we have little
> of ourselves left for ourselves. And whatever anger we might
> feel—at society, at our husband, at the experts who led us
> to this pass—is directed, also, at ourselves. Or at the one
> permissible target: other mothers.

Physical Self-Esteem—When we don't manage our weight, or when we let ourselves go in general, we are setting ourselves up for poor self-esteem. And, believe me, I do understand the problem. I gained huge amounts of weight with each of my children, including nearly 50 (yes, you read that right, Five Oh) pounds with my third child.

During my fourth pregnancy, a young female instructor at my kids' karate class asked me how I felt. My response was, "Fat, thank you." With the same horror and fascination a child might have on discovering a dead snake, she scrunched her nose but continued to probe, "Does this always happen when you're pregnant?"

"Yup, this is how I do pregnancy—big and fat." She flinched.

See, I'm the poster girl for how NOT to do pregnancies. I get so fat that I have to beg my husband to have sex with me (he'll deny it, but it's true). Tim likes to joke that I become so big, I develop my own gravitational field (which also explains how all that food gets on my shirts). When I discovered I was pregnant with our fourth, I felt it my duty to warn my new neighbors about the incredible weight gain to come. I suggested they close their blinds lest I scare their children during the rapid transformation. So, yeah, I get fat.

But I also believe in trying to lose that weight once the baby arrives. If I'm already struggling to feel good about myself, the last thing I need is a weight problem. So I waddle my oversized rear end to the gym and endure the patronizing comments from instructors and other students who naturally assume from the looks of my body that I've never worked out a day in my life.

When Operation Iraqi Freedom was launched, Rhonda's husband began spending more time in the Middle East than at home. It was at this point that Rhonda decided it was time to leave her career. She says this about exercise:

I've boosted my self-esteem by spending time in the gym,
not only working on my physical body but also working out

*frustrations from home that I have a hard time controlling.
When you are working in an office environment, sometimes
it is easier to side-step problems or even ask for assistance
or guidance. As a stay-at-home mom, and essentially a single
mom now that my husband is overseas, I can't walk away
from problems at home or even find assistance in some cases.
You can turn a computer off, but you can't turn off a child,
especially when dinner is burning, the phone is ringing, the dog
is chewing things, and the wash is overflowing. I have found if I
spend time working out, I not only look better, but I feel better
and have better control of my response in difficult situations.*

For women, an often overlooked aspect about exercise is that it
can truly make us strong. Perhaps I'm odd, but I like to lift heavy objects.
Sometimes, I pretend that I'm at Venice Beach and flex my muscles in
front of the mirror: ARRR! I can push large boulders, move heavy pieces of
furniture, and even carry my child from the parking lot to the store in one
of those baby carriers that weighs a ton. Being a strong woman is cool.

Messages from the Media—Over the years, the family-unfriendly
message has increased to the point that it can no longer be ignored as an
occasional exception. Some of us have become so numb to these messages
that we no longer recognize when our own values have been attacked.

Sometimes, these unhelpful messages can be found in the lyrics of
our favorite songs. I was driving down the road a while back when I became
aware that I was singing along to the radio. The tune playing was Reba
McEntire's "Is There Life Out There?" I probably would never have realized
what I was doing had it not been for the sudden feeling of discontent that
came over me. I wanted to run, to escape my life. I wanted out. It took me a
minute to realize that the lyrics I was singing voiced these exact sentiments.

If you examine the words to this song, you can easily see why I found myself feeling the way I did: a disenchanted housewife finds herself wondering about the value of the life she is living and what she may have missed by marrying and having children at a young age. The song goes on to ask if she should do what she is daring herself—presumably to leave her family.

How would such a song make you feel? To be truthful, it makes me want to give Reba a piece of my mind. Sure, I understand she's reflecting a sentiment that we certainly all can relate to occasionally; but, by golly, I don't need to hear it. I want to stay focused and on task. I need to be edified not weakened. The last thing I need right now is to sing along with "Ode to Me" ballads. I can only wonder how many women packed their bags and ditched their families after hearing that song.

But just as music has the power to bring us down, it also has power to raise us up. I heard Phil Vassar's melody, "Just Another Day in Paradise," some time later. If you're familiar with this popular country-western ballad, you'll recall the story line: a man reflects on the frustrating chaos within his home, what with the kids crying, a pile of past-due bills waiting to be paid, dog out of control, appliances in disrepair, and food gone sour in the fridge. Probably sounds familiar, but not terribly encouraging, right? However, the tune quickly shifts gears, and you see the man recognizing that his relationship with his spouse and children is much deeper and far more important than the superficial challenges that come with the package. He sees two hearts and one dream, something that he is grateful for, and he finds that there is no other place that he'd rather be.

What a different effect this song had on my psyche. Instead of wanting to leave my screaming kids at the side of the road, this song reframed the craziness of my life. It helped me instead to appreciate this special and unique time in my life, one that passes by surprisingly quickly.

Getting Proactive

In addition to defending ourselves from unwanted attacks on our self-worth, we can take proactive steps to improve our self-esteem.

Evaluate Your Self-Talk—You may not be aware of it, but each minute of the day, you are engaged in conversation with yourself. Sometimes the conversation is of a practical nature: "I need to get to the meeting by 6:00 PM" or "Johnny is probably grumpy because he hasn't had a nap." But at other times, the conversation can simply be expressive: "How could I be so stupid!" or "How could I forget that appointment?"

More than likely, you're not even aware of most of the dialogue passing through your mind, so stop and listen. "I can't take this anymore!" in all of its variations is the message I often hear in my head and that sometimes even reaches my lips. When we catch a self-berating message, we need to replace the negative with something empowering and positive, such as, "I can handle this!"

The vocabulary we choose can also affect our self-esteem.

Examples of words to forget include:

> I CAN'T
>
> I SHOULD HAVE
>
> IF ONLY
>
> IT'S TOO DIFFICULT
>
> I'M STRESSED

Example of words to use include:

> I CAN
>
> I WILL

NEXT TIME

IT'S A CHALLENGING OPPORTUNITY

I'M MOTIVATED

Whether the messages are negative mental reruns from the past or our own masochistic twist on self-deprecation, we need to be aware of them and replace them with healthy, uplifting ones.

Accomplish Something—One of the quickest ways to boost your self-esteem is to accomplish something tangible. Whether it's a creative outlet, a hobby, a home business, or a volunteer effort, when you feel you have accomplished something, at the end of the day you'll feel better about yourself.

Sometimes, our situation is such that it can be difficult for us to leave our homes. In this instance, it becomes necessary to find activities we can do from our home to challenge our creative intellect. Over the years, I've refinished tables, reupholstered the chairs, wallpapered my dining room, antiqued my lighting fixtures, and faux painted my kitchen. My home is a far cry from a domestic refuge, but each of these projects was intrinsically rewarding.

Stay True to Yourself—I probably don't need to say this, but I will. Self-worth also comes from being a person of integrity, making choices that are virtuous and morally uplifting. It's hard to like yourself if you are frequently ugly to your husband or if you are engaged in an activity that is contrary to your beliefs. Unless one is a sociopath, morality, integrity, and responsibility are essential to positive self-worth.

Be Patient—Leaving your career to raise your family is an enormous step, and a change of this magnitude can wreak havoc on your self-esteem. But with patience, you will see that, over time, your self-esteem not only adjusts, it also becomes more robust.

As Nietzsche reminds us, "That which does not kill us makes us stronger." Leaving your career to raise your children will not kill you, of course, but it does present a significant challenge. And that challenge, if you let it, will make you very strong, indeed.

CHAPTER 6

The Challenge of Parenting

*There are only two ways to live
your life. One is as though nothing
is a miracle. The other is as though
everything is a miracle.*

~Albert Einstein

All parents notice very early on that their children are miraculously complex beings with seemingly endless cognitive, emotional, and development potential. Along with these endless possibilities, however, comes the awesome responsibility of helping your little miracle reach his or her full potential.

So, despite whatever personal issues you may be working through with respect to your career, or how many loads of laundry you need to fold, parenting becomes, by default, your most important occupation. For those new to child rearing, I've included this chapter to assist you with the transition from your former career into what will, at first, appear to be a very foreign line of work. I encourage you to use this material as a launching point for further study.

The Baby Stage

You may never revisit a time more adorable than the baby stage. Those chubby cheeks, innocent eyes, and toothless smiles—it all just makes you want to gobble them up! But with the delightful cuteness come challenges that catch many new parents off guard. This stage is often more difficult for a parent because the demands babies impose are relentless, and their behavior can be so mysterious.

Tim and I experienced much anxiety during the baby stage. We were afraid that our babies could die suddenly in their sleep, get cancer from eating toothpaste, swan dive from the top stair, choke on a grape, fry at an electrical outlet, or drown in the toilet. Whether it was going out to dinner, visiting friends, or hanging out at the mall, we were always on edge, never knowing when our trip might be aborted prematurely by something frustratingly unpredictable, like a diaper blowout, or unnerving, like the occasional near-death experience.

We recently came across a photo that was taken at the hospital when our third child was born. On the delivery bed sits our oldest, who had just turned three; our middle son, who had yet to turn two; and our brand-new baby daughter. We look at that picture and wonder to this day how we could have survived that stage of life.

Probably the most important thing to remember about the baby stage is that it is just that, a stage. Within this period, as with all life stages, are individual phases, some wonderful, others decidedly not. Although the baby stage and some of its phases can feel overwhelming, my experience has been that the stress level becomes significantly less as the baby grows into childhood. Of course, this may be of little consolation to you right now if those easier days seem years away. And while I can't offer you the full respite you probably need, I can offer suggestions to help smooth the edges during this unique and sometimes challenging time. What follows are a few basics from my professional experience and the lessons that Tim and I learned with our own children.

Attachment Parenting versus Parent-Guided Parenting—
Among the many common parenting controversies—breast-versus-bottle,

working-versus-nonworking mothers, and so on—is the debate between advocates of attachment parenting and those of parent-guided parenting. Tim and I are advocates of parent-guided parenting.

One of the parent-guided principles that Tim and I adopted with our firstborn was establishing a flexible feeding and nap schedule. Flexible scheduling helped our babies learn to eat and sleep at generally predictable times of day. By gently nudging our babies into a repetitive schedule, Tim and I were able to assure that their basic needs for nourishment and rest were met while reestablishing some order in our lives.

We found that a well-rested and well-nourished baby increased the probability that he or she would have a happy disposition. Knowing approximately when our babies were scheduled to eat and sleep proved invaluable when deciphering the cause of their tears. Flexible scheduling also helped our children establish good nighttime sleep habits, which they continue to enjoy to this day.

Some advocates of attachment parenting encourage mothers to hold their babies virtually all of their waking hours. In my opinion, this is an unreasonable expectation to place on a mother and almost impossible to continue after the birth of the second child. While touch and responsiveness to your baby are both critical to good parenting, there is no harm done in occasionally allowing a baby to romp in a bouncer or play alone on the carpet with a few toys.

Whatever path you choose, exercise sound judgment while attending to the individual needs of your baby and family. This is more important than adhering to one particular philosophy.

Sleep Props—Sleep props are items or habits that become conditioned into the normal activity of sleeping. Feeding or rocking your baby to sleep, a favorite blanket, or even providing absolute silence in the house while baby rests are all examples of sleep props.

The problem with props is that they become necessary for sleep. Some parents don't mind this; they enjoy the special time rocking or feeding their baby before a nap. But keep in mind that if you condition your child with a prop at bedtime, you may be setting the stage for trouble later, particularly when it comes time to wean your child from his prop. The first time your mother-in-law watches your baby, she may have an overwhelming time putting the baby down for a nap if she doesn't know the exact routine or doesn't have the proper "equipment."

With the exception of their favorite blankets, all of our children learned to sleep without props as babies. After their goodnight kiss, we'd lay them in the crib—almost always without tears or incident, even in unfamiliar environments. Again, you should perform the approach you use with flexibility and discernment, taking into consideration the unique needs of each child and the particular situation.

Touch—All humans need touch, and this is particularly true for infants. According to the University of Miami, touch has been shown to facilitate weight gain in preterm infants, reduce stress hormones, alleviate symptoms of depression, reduce pain, improve immune function, and alter brain function in the direction of heightened awareness.

Our babies' need for touch does not necessitate that we hold them all day long; but it does require that we remain continuously attentive to this area of their development. For many, cuddling and caressing our baby on a regular basis will be a natural instinct that requires no further discussion. For others, particularly those who may not have received much physical touch as a child or who suffered from abuse, it may be necessary to remind yourselves to spend time touching and holding your baby.

Older children need to be touched, too, of course. In this case, though, it can be a little more challenging, because they rarely seem to slow down. I make it a point to regularly touch my children's heads and shoulders, or to finagle them into giving me an occasional hug. Touch is an essential human need, so we want to make sure that our kids are getting plenty of healthy touch and never feel like they have to seek it outside the home.

Toddlers and Beyond

A significant portion of our personality is formed during the first five years of life. Here are some of the basics that will help you create a healthy environment for the development of your child's personality. Note that all of them require your continued vigilance and ongoing active involvement during the process.

Security and Consistency—You have the power to impart to your child a sense of security, stability, and trust. Simple routines, including meals, bath time, nap time, and story time, will help your child learn to trust. A sense of security at home will form the foundation for the confidence your child will eventually need to face the world. While many of these tasks may feel mundane and pointless to you now, remember that you don't necessarily have to enjoy them for their value to transcend generations.

Educational Goals—As the primary caregiver for your child, it is your job to ensure that your child meets his or her early cognitive and developmental needs. The entrance requirements for the average kindergarten class are generally not exceptionally demanding, which means it really doesn't take more than a modest amount of effort on your part to ensure that your child is prepared. Most schools are happy to tell you what they expect from your child at the time of enrollment. The educator within me began calling schools when my first son was only two years old; I wanted to be sure I was preparing him properly. The widespread availability of preschool workbooks, part-time preschool programs, and fun educational computer games can help ease this task.

While you may think your child will be better prepared for kindergarten by first enrolling him or her in a preschool program, keep in mind that success is not always guaranteed. Case in point is a story told to me by a friend and full-time working mother. The preschool that had cared for her daughter since birth boasted of a kindergarten readiness program. It wasn't until after her daughter failed her public school kindergarten readiness exam that my friend learned that her daughter had not been prepared adequately. While there are some wonderful curricula that can help assure our children are prepared for kindergarten, we should not forget that the ultimate responsibility for this mission falls on our shoulders.

Advocacy—Another important task of parenting is advocacy. Parents serve as advocates when they work to ensure that their children's individual needs are met. As my child's advocate, my job is to push. I pushed to ensure that my kids had the opportunity to attend the best public school. I pushed to have my kids tested for the gifted program. I pushed to obtain in-school speech therapy for my son.

Advocacy is a lot like removing choking brush from a trail. We help clear the way so our kids can continue with their already demanding journey without being unnecessarily encumbered by tangles and poky bushes. This isn't a case of vicarious parenting, where parents live through their offspring, expecting them to excel strictly for the parent's own ego gratification. It also doesn't imply having an attitude that makes our children's teachers want to run and hide when they see us coming.

Many parents don't realize just how powerful they are. Remember that you have rights! Most organizations, such as your child's pediatric office or school, have tucked away in the corner drawer a document containing rights and policies that pertain to you as a parent.

Sometimes, you'll find an intimidating gorilla sitting in the receptionist chair working hard to keep you from getting this information. But most organizations actually have very parent-friendly policies. If you feel that for some reason your child is not receiving the services or attention he or she is entitled to, request a copy of the organization's policy to better understand and exercise your rights.

I was once employed part time for a private children's psychiatric hospital and often observed the dynamics between the children's guardians and the staff. While it was often the case that dysfunctional parents were the source of the child's problem, this wasn't always true. Frequently, it was healthy parents, grandparents, or foster parents who cared for the child. Guardians would ask the hospital staff, "What kind of medications is my child on?" "How did she get this bruise?" or "What did you feed him for dinner?" All are legitimate questions.

But many of the staff found these queries annoying. Instead of viewing such involvement as an indication of healthy parenting, they considered it a nuisance or an insult to their professional judgment. "I am not going to speak to that nosy mother!" a nurse might bark before a meeting with parents. "Why does that obsessive father keep calling me?" The exchanges between concerned parents and staff often became highly charged or confrontational.

Unfortunately, the mind-set that I observed at the hospital can be found just about anywhere. For years, I'd let people intimidate me, not real-izing the basic rule that bullies only bully the timid. Now if someone wants to be put out because I refuse to relinquish my role as advocate for my chil-dren, that person can expect confrontation with a determined parent.

It is your job to advocate and assure that your child's needs are met. If you tend to be shy, remember, the more you practice being assertive, the more quickly you will actually become so. In the meantime, fake it until you make it.

Discipline and Moral Guidance

Regardless of the appearance of your kitchen or the origin of the offensive smell coming from the laundry room, your most important parenting mission can be summed up as this: to do all that you can to shape and direct your child's conscience and personality so that he or she might someday become a person of integrity. High grades, an impressive resume, an expansive portfolio—each has tangible value. But they are meaningless in an adult without moral principles.

Discipline is essential to the formation of a healthy conscience, a firm sense of self, and a life of integrity. However, some perceive discipline as distasteful and unnecessary. I encountered an extreme example of this in a young woman I met at a birthing class. She had been taught in college that saying no to a child would quench his or her spirit. She insisted that, because all children are inherently good, they never require punishment. Some may recognize this philosophy as an element of Carl Rogers's humanistic theory, the belief that all people begin life basically good, but it's the world that screws them up. Most adherents to this theory usually cut up their membership card after they become parents and their innocent little sweet pea starts biting the pet, tossing plates, and hitting grandma.

Despite my attempts to convince this woman that she was about to make a very serious mistake, my advice fell on deaf ears. It was three years later that I received the follow-up report from a mutual acquaintance: my classmate's son had indeed become nothing less than an incorrigible little monster. So horrible, in fact, that no sitter would return to watch him a second time.

Teaching your child boundaries is common sense to most people. But many new parents, insecure about their unfamiliar role, will latch onto the first expert opinion they stumble across, particularly if the title "Doctor" graces the authority's name. Some popular theories are truly bizarre and run counter to instinctual wisdom, confirming that those who devise them must have had no children of their own to prove them wrong!

Like it or not, life is full of boundaries. We must stop when the light turns red, pay our taxes, respect the orders of our superiors, and go to the end of the line. These are the characteristics of a person with integrity, an individual who meets his or her own goals but within the framework of moral and social norms.

Compare this to the characteristics of sociopaths, who lack self-regulation, believe they are above the law, and constantly overindulge themselves. If you teach your children that there is no such thing as "no," you are fostering in them the foundational characteristics of a sociopath.

Instead, teach your children to exhibit control within a fixed moral framework. Be consistent and firm in correcting them when you see them deviating from the path you know they should be on. Ensure that they understand the reason for your use of correction: It is based on your sincere love and concern for their current and future well-being.

Curbing the Tantrums

Tantrums are another issue that parents often fail to address. Tantrums happen. How you respond to them is key to how long you will have to deal with them. If you reinforce them, not only can you expect that your children will not grow out of them, but you can also expect them to become increasingly more difficult to control. By the time your children have reached their teens, they will have mastered the art of manipulation, manifested as passive-aggressive behavior, active rebellion, direct aggression, and, in some cases, suicidal gestures.

Children become psychiatric patients for three primary reasons. The first is that they may have a biological or medical source for their mental illness. The second is that they may have suffered abuse and are acting out as a result of the pain. But the third reason is the result of a normal parent who was simply too nice. When the four-year-old child tossed his plate to the floor, Dad said, "Let's talk about your feelings." When the six-year-old didn't get a new bike for Christmas and threw herself into a rage, Grandma said, "Don't worry. We can buy you one tomorrow!"

By the time these children become teenagers, the manipulation has advanced to the point that the parent is no longer able to control them. "I'm going to kill myself if you don't let me go out with Andy!" a daughter might scream. If Mom says no, the angry daughter runs to the medicine cabinet and proceeds to swallow the contents of a bottle of painkillers. After her stomach is pumped, she is sent to the psychiatric hospital, where her new life as a mental patient begins.

I once sat in a therapy session with a mother of one of these children. The mother appeared very normal. She was of average weight, well dressed, well spoken, educated, and pleasant. Her daughter, on the other hand, was overweight, over-pierced, and overindulged. "You forgot to bring my nail polish!" the daughter screamed at her mother from across the room. For over 10 minutes, the daughter's accusations of seemingly petty infractions continued. Since it was obvious we weren't going to make progress with this type of behavior, I sent the daughter back to her unit. When I was alone with the mother, I asked her why she tolerated her child yelling at her in this manner. She smiled, and with a tone of pride in her voice, acknowledged, "I've always let her talk to me that way. We're best friends."

Trying to be friends with your children makes for out-of-control kids who neither respect nor truly like you. Your job right now is to be a parent. Someday, you may also develop a deep friendship with your child, but that will only happen after respect has been established.

Styles of Parenting

Diana Baumrind, who studied parenting styles in the United States, concluded that 77 percent of families fell into one of three parenting styles:

Authoritarian. Parents have an established set of rules they use to control and shape their children's behavior. They stress the need for obedience and use punishment to reduce misbehavior.

Authoritative. Parents explain the rules and are willing to listen to their children's point of view, but they may not accept it. They are not as likely to use physical punishment and are less likely to stress absolute obedience.

Permissive. Parents demonstrate less control over their children, either because they feel the children need to learn from their own experiences or because they don't want the bother of disciplining their children. Their schedules are loose, they demand less of their children, and they are more likely to tolerate immature behavior.

Baumrind's research found that children of authoritarian parents tended to be less friendly, less sociable, and more withdrawn. Children of the more permissive style of parenting were more likely to be moody, immature, dependent, and demonstrate low self-control. The children of authoritative parents, on the other hand, tended to be well liked, possessed good social skills, and were cooperative and more independent. In essence, the research suggests that we should establish our authority as parents, but at the same time use sound judgment, demonstrate flexibility, and be willing to acknowledge when we are wrong.

What You Reinforce Will Return

Behaviors or misbehaviors, when reinforced, eventually return. Reinforcement can take the form of anything from a lollipop, to a positive word, to much-needed attention.

When my baby throws a tantrum, there are essentially three responses I can choose from; two of them decrease the likelihood that the behavior will return; the third reinforces, or increases, its probability. Ignoring the inappropriate behavior (a process called extinction) and punishment are the two ways I can reduce the likelihood of the recurrence of a particular behavior. Eliminating an inappropriate behavior is a process that happens over time and requires consistency. Since my son is still a baby, my preferred method is to simply ignore—that is, to extinguish—the inappropriate behavior.

Strangers, often well meaning, can inadvertently reinforce bad behavior. On several occasions, when one of my children was behaving inappropriately in public, a stranger offered a treat to help calm him or her. From the perspective of eliminating a negative behavior, this can be quite dangerous. Positive reinforcement of an undesirable behavior, even if it only occurs once, practically guarantees that the behavior will recur. I've had to stop many a kind-hearted person from screwing up my hard work. Those five minutes of peace can cost me months of bad behavior. They look at me like I'm nuts for refusing their offers to placate my children, but I'm a therapist, for crying out loud! Because it takes so little to reinforce bad behavior, on the days when one of my children has been particularly difficult, I try to be grateful for the simple fact that I was the one there to handle the problem.

Reward and Punish in Close Proximity to the Behavior— Reward and punishment are more effective the closer in time they follow the behavior at issue. This is particularly true for younger children. I was at the community pool recently and overheard a mother attempting to convince her four-year-old daughter to come out of the water. When the child didn't respond, the mother threatened to take 10 minutes from her swimming time on their next visit to the pool. The child didn't budge. Why?

There are a couple of problems with this mother's approach. First, a child that young is probably unable to grasp the concept of visiting the pool "the next time." You might as well be talking to her about the year of her college graduation. The second problem is that Mom will most likely forget that she took 10 minutes off pool time on their next visit. So, in effect, there is likely to be no effective punishment for the child's disobedience. But let's say Mom does indeed remember the penalty the next time they go to the pool. Is she really going to feel like punishing her daughter, knowing the tears and protest it will cause? At the time of the infraction, she actually had only two viable options after physically removing her daughter from the pool: to use some form of physical punishment or to take away another privilege as soon as possible.

Teaching Our Children the Value of Work—Just because I'm the soul of the household doesn't imply that I'm the servant, too. Okay, when my children were very young, yes, I admit I was indeed the indentured servant. But I understood that this was just a phase and that our children someday would be expected to participate in the business of running the household. And as they have grown older, they have, indeed, assumed an increasing share of the chores required to keep our home afloat. Their level of participation, of course, has depended on their ages.

Before age two, we'd occasionally sing a "clean-up" song with our children; but, of course, Tim and I would do most of the work ourselves. By the time each reached four years old, however, our expectations had grown, and our children were required to straighten their rooms. Today, at ages ten, eight, and six, our three oldest children help with the dishes, wipe the counters, vacuum and mop the floors, clean baseboards, match socks, sweep the porch, fold their own laundry, and feed the cats. I don't expect that all of these chores be performed every day because our children's primary job is to be good students. But the intent has been to establish, at an early age, the expectation that everyone, not just Mom and Dad, participates in household chores.

I've also unilaterally decided that I will not be one of those poor women who spend each "holiday" a complete wreck trying to cook and clean while the rest of the family sits on the couch watching football. I, too, would like to enjoy each holiday celebration. I actually made this decision several years ago at a friend's party. My friend was hosting her own Mother's Day celebration, and her grown children were in attendance. During the party, her son presented her with a card. I still remember what it said: "On Mother's Day, YOU deserve to be pampered!"

So far so good, you might think. But after handing Mom the card, son quickly retreated, only to be seen momentarily at dinner. And for the rest of the evening, it was the mothers who cooked, set the table, and cleaned up afterward. This window into the future depressed me. Could I really be destined for perpetual servitude with no hope of truly being appreciated, even on Mother's Day? I decided then that the correct answer was no.

Teaching a child to be a part of the operating system of a family begins at an early age. I imagine that career moms have an easier time recognizing this, because they simply can't do everything in the limited time available at the end of the day. But those of us at home might make the mistake of thinking all the chores at home are our duty and feel guilty even considering asking our children for help. Think again.

Sociologists Scott Coltrane and Michele Adams from the University of California at Riverside discovered that school-age children who do chores with their fathers get along better with peers and have more friends. They also found that they are less likely to disobey teachers or cause trouble at school and are happier and more outgoing.

Keep in mind that you are raising a future spouse or parent. What you teach your children about the division of chores will be carried with them into their own families. So, get started early. Your role in life is not to be a pathetic martyr. If you'd like to teach your son to never lift a hand once he is married, then do everything for him now. If you want to suggest to your daughter that being a stay-at-home mother is dreary and dirty work, do everything for her today. However, if you'd rather teach your kids that a family needs to work together to serve each other, then give them age-appropriate tasks as soon as they are able to handle them.

We once visited with a friend who had a strong opinion of how dishes should be stacked. I was trying to help her by loading the dishwasher. "Oh no, that plate doesn't go there!" she'd yell. I'd laugh, and, with exaggerated effort, attempt to place another item in the dishwasher, only to watch her anxiety build. It was hilarious as she desperately tried to rein in her need for control.

We all have issues that can drive us nuts; my friend's just happened to involve her dishwasher. But we need to ask ourselves whether our obsessive issues are really that important. With the thousands of times that dishes will be run through that dishwasher, does it really matter if plates sit on the left-hand side instead of the right during one or two wash cycles? If we aren't willing to let go of our need for perfection, we're destined to carry the burden of household chores full time and forever.

As an example of letting go, our boys started folding their own laundry at about age six. The trick has been to avoid looking into their drawer afterward. I hope, over time, they'll begin to take more pride in keeping it clean. But I figure if they want a crappy-looking drawer, they can have a crappy-looking drawer. As long as they can close the drawer, I don't care.

So, when you give your children chores, understand that they won't be able to perform them to your standards, at least not initially. Let go of your need for perfection. I feel that an 80 percent clean floor is better than a 100 percent dirty floor. Decide what areas don't require perfection and make these your children's tasks. Compliment them repeatedly for exceptional effort and tell them how much you appreciate their help. Reward your children's hard work with positive feedback, a regular allowance, computer time, or other incentives.

Consider the Past

Never underestimate the impact that your own childhood experiences might have on your own parenting style. Factors such as family traditions, religious convictions, abuse, and your parents' approach to raising children are all relevant to your current experience.

Interpreting the influence of past abuse is a particularly difficult task. The effects of abuse can vary tremendously, and I could fill an entire book by matching forms of abuse to outcome possibilities. If you suffered from either physical or mental abuse, you may have to work especially hard to counter any of the negative patterns you learned. Here are a few examples of how abuse might manifest itself:

- A person who grew up in a dysfunctional home and was never exposed to appropriate parenting may find herself at a complete loss when trying to determine what healthy parenting is.

- Someone who was raised by an excessively domineering or physically abusive parent may move to the opposite extreme and take a hands-off approach to his child's misbehaviors.

- An individual who experienced ongoing food issues during childhood, ranging from too little food to too much, might find that the same issues resurface when it comes to feeding her own family.

- A parent who was once psychologically manipulated by means of head games may find herself repeating these same games with her own children.

- Past sexual abuse is the most common cause of the next generation of predators. Sexual abuse can also lead to serious trust issues.

These are just a few of many possible scenarios that can occur with parents who were abused as children. If you were abused as a child, there are many resources available that can help you explore your own parenting dynamics. In some cases, particularly if you've experienced extreme forms of abuse, you may find it beneficial to seek counseling.

You are obviously not disqualified as a good parent just because you might have suffered abuse in the past. But past abuse does suggest that you may need to be more on guard against repeating unhealthy patterns or swinging the pendulum too far in the direction of leniency. Never view yourself as damaged; instead, focus on the many lessons you've learned along the way. And remember this anonymous quote: Every flower grows through dirt.

They're Watching!

I really wanted to skip this section because of my own failures in this area, but the bottom line is that our kids are always watching and learning from us. They not only listen to our words, but they cross-check these against our actions as well. Joanne, an occupational therapist and mother of four, sums this up nicely: "Having those wide eyes watching and little mouths repeating my words has been a humbling experience when the less-than-flattering aspects of my personality have been imitated."

Speak in Glowing Terms—Tim and I have great kids. I suppose that some of this comes from genetics, some from our hard work, much from divine interference, and some simply because they aren't yet teenagers. Whatever the collective reason, we've been blessed with wonderful kids.

Unfortunately, I haven't always admitted to it. Until recently, I had the bad habit of presenting the counter position to compliments directed at my children. If a teacher said, "Your child is so well behaved" I might have responded with, "Yeah, well you should see him at home!" And while it's true my children do generally behave worse at home, the fact that they were behaving well at school was still a great thing to hear. But I realize now that this negative comeback reflex was actually an old habit with roots in my own low self-esteem. Even to this day, whenever I receive a compliment, I am quick to put myself down. I simply generalized this habitual response to my children. Now that I am aware of it, and am more cognizant of the fact that my kids are often listening, I have been working to respond more positively.

Sometimes strangers will introduce the "aren't kids the pits?" topic into a conversation. I was shopping one day when a sales clerk approached me and, after cooing at my baby, inquired, "Has anyone told you about teenagers yet? They suck!" Comments such as this one are common, and my tendency was always to laugh or add one of my own equally flip remarks. When I appear ready to throttle my kids because of their behavior, I often hear things like, "I bet you can't wait for summer to be over!" "Yeah," I used to say, "I'm counting the days. Won't be long! Woo hoo!"

But all those laughs at my kids' expense stopped one day after a similar exchange when I saw my oldest son looking up at me with a very sad expression. Later he asked, "Mom, do you like when we're home for summer?" It broke my heart. Now, when someone wants to start the "aren't kids the pits" jokes, I don't participate. It doesn't ease the agony of trying to shop with four young kids, and I may come off as a little snobby to some. But that's far better than hurting my kids' feelings by making statements I don't really mean.

Laugh—Are you laughing with your children? Sometimes I find myself so busy with all the craziness of life that I miss opportunities to have a good chuckle with my kids. My baby loves when I tickle his face with my hair, but so many of our diaper changes are just acts of drudgery instead of moments of fun. My daughter jumps for joy when I join her for a good Celtic dance in the living room, but I always have so much to do. I can easily cheer up my middle son with a bear hug and a tickle, but I sometimes forget that. And my oldest loves a good joke, but I'm so busy taking life too seriously that I miss the humor.

I try to lighten up because I know how important laughter is to family bonding. It is by far the easiest way to connect with your child in his world. Laughter breaks tension, heals wounds, and strengthens the parent-child relationship. We could all use a little bit more of it.

Establishing Healthy Eating and Exercise Patterns—It's no secret that obesity is reaching epidemic proportions in our children. Results from the 1999–2002 National Health and Nutrition Examination Survey (NHANES) revealed that 16 percent of children ages six to 19 are overweight. This represents a 45 percent increase over the last survey period (1988–94).

In their 2002 report. "Maternal Employment and Overweight Children," Patricia Anderson, Kristin Butcher, and Phillip Levine discuss a study sponsored by the Federal Reserve Bank of Chicago that revealed that "a child is more likely to be overweight if his/her mother worked more hours per week over the child's life. Analyses by subgroups show that it is higher socioeconomic status mothers whose work intensity is particularly deleterious for their child's overweight status."

As our children's primary caregiver, we have the opportunity to assure that our children eat healthy food and get the exercise they need. Let's face it. Most food targeted at children is deplorable. Children need to be exposed to healthy food at a very young age; and we, as parents, need to work hard to control the garbage intake.

I have known many educated women who seem to lack real concern or power when it comes to their kids' food choices. I met a dietician who claimed her seven-year-old son would eat nothing but pizza, and a pediatric nurse who packed her son's lunch bag every day with peanut butter cookies, snack crackers, pastry, and Kool-Aid because he refused to eat anything else. Teaching our children to enjoy a variety of healthy foods starts now.

Tim and I have consistently exposed our children to outdoor activities, not only because they are so intrinsically healthful and rewarding, but also in the hope that they will someday adopt them as their own. We've taken them on innumerable day hikes, beach swims, and camping excursions. They've backpacked on the Appalachian Trail, canoed in the Canadian wilderness, and hiked in the Mojave Desert and High Sierra. Staying fit isn't just about being a participant in organized sports, especially those that are unlikely to be available to them when they are adults. It is, instead, a lifestyle that incorporates exercise into the joy of living. The wonderful memories are a fringe benefit.

Respect the Unique Nature of Your Child

Children are truly unique creatures. Each contains the genetic makeup not only of both of his or her parents, but also grandparents and all the generations before them. This means that your child is not simply a product of you and your spouse, but a composite of many. Billions of people have walked on this planet, yet no one shares even your child's fingerprint. He or she is a rare creature indeed.

This being the case, just because Dad might have been an exceptional softball player, doesn't mean his son is. Simply because you love musicals doesn't guarantee this passion will be passed on to your child. There is nothing wrong with encouraging your children to explore in a particular direction, as long as you respect the individual nature of your child. Parents with weak egos may attempt to feed their own through the lives of their children. At a time when our own egos might be weak following our departure from our career, we have to be cautious to keep our own identity separate from that of our child's.

Limit Television

I admit it. I have a love-hate relationship with television. I wish television were what it was when I was growing up; but, unfortunately, it is not. Television is becoming increasingly more violent, vulgar, and sexually explosive. Tim and I castigated our television for years, turning it off for long periods, hoping that it would come back to us someday like the Prodigal Son, repenting of its evil ways and returning to a life of decency. But it only got worse.

The final betrayal came one morning many years ago when I placed my two angelic toddlers in front of the screen to watch *Sesame Street*. I turned on the TV and walked away. Only it wasn't *Sesame Street*. I had accidentally moved the channel to Jerry Springer. I whirled around and raced back to change the station. But in the mere matter of seconds that it took me to cross the room, I watched a woman walk up on stage and rip off her shirt behind a caption that flashed "I LOVE TO HAVE SEX!" My children were too young to read, and they probably thought the lady must have been getting ready to take a bath, but I was shocked. On one channel, my children could practice their ABCs, on the other, they could learn the fine art of being white trash. So that was the end of network and cable television in our home. Today, we only use the TV set to watch movies on DVD or play video games.

A lot of people think we are absolutely nuts. Some even argue with us that we are depriving our children in some way. People have asked, "But how will your children ever learn about the real world?" If television properly represents the real world, we're all in serious trouble.

According to the National Institute for Mental Health (NIMH), "Commercial television for children is 50 to 60 times more violent than prime time programs for adults; some cartoons average 80 violent acts per hour." We were on a road trip recently, watching television from our beds one evening in our hotel room. Tim and I allowed our kids to fall asleep to a children's network, but I continued to watch. I noticed that the network seemed to suddenly switch its target audience from the five- to 12-year-old age group to those much older. One minute, we were watching Jimmy Neutron; the next, I was watching Roseanne. The producers picked an interesting episode for their older "target" audience. The drama that evening highlighted Roseanne's daughter and her first sexual experience with her boyfriend.

According to the American Academy of Pediatrics (AAP), the average child watches about four hours of television each day. By the time these children finish grade school, they will have viewed approximately 8,000 simulated murders. If you don't think this is significant, consider that "fifty percent of murder victims are between 15 and 34 years old; and 55 percent of those arrested for murder are under 25 years old."

The National Institute of Mental Health goes on to state: "In magnitude, exposure to television violence is as strongly correlated with aggressive behavior as any other behavioral variable that has been measured."

Researchers revealed in the April 2004 issue of *Pediatrics* that, for every hour each day that preschoolers watch TV, they also increase their probability of developing attention deficit problems later in life by an additional 10 percent. Increased television viewing is also correlated with obesity. Lounging in front of the TV is potentially time that could have been spent playing outdoors.

The AAP recommends that children under age two completely abstain from watching television and that older children only be allowed to watch or play one to two hours of television or videos games each day. Of course, content during this time should also be screened carefully.

Down Time—Children need time without television, video games, and structured lessons. They need time to dig in the dirt, to invent, to pretend, to read, and to simply experience the wonders of life. Overstimulated kids become overstimulation–seekers, constantly looking outside themselves for the next rush. Don't be afraid to let your children suffer from boredom from time to time. Let them learn how to entertain themselves in healthy and creative ways.

Accept Humility

A beautiful thing about parenting is that it can keep you humble. If you're feeling particularly proud of your children's dinner manners on Monday, you can be sure that they'll let go a rip-roaring belch at the restaurant on Tuesday. Truth is, they'll find all sorts of creative ways to embarrass you. They'll pee in your neighbor's bushes during the ladies' lunchtime tea; they'll loudly announce the physical faults of an approaching stranger; and, as every parent of a teenager can tell you, they can royally screw up. Maintaining a sense of humor and keeping your own identity separate from your children's will help you weather the storms along the way.

The Mantle of Parenthood

One of the more interesting perspectives on parenting comes from actor and director Jodie Foster. Regardless of what you might think of her mysterious childbearing methods, you have to respect the manner in which she reprioritized her life. To spend more time with her children, Foster, according to an April 2002 article in *People Weekly,* closed down her 12-year-old production company and limits her acting jobs to one film every two years. Her philosophical rationale has stuck with me from the day I read it: "Some actors pay someone to walk their dog and pick up the kids from school," she said. "But that's your life. So you're paying someone else to live your life so you can work more? I'd rather pay somebody to work for me."

Let's be honest. Parenting isn't easy. The job is often stressful, frustrating, dirty, and rarely appreciated. But, as Ms. Foster reminds us, this is your life; and you've left your career to live it more fully. The good and the bad, the laughter and the sorrow, it is uniquely yours. Embrace it.

CHAPTER 7

Marriage Transformation

Success in marriage does not come
merely through finding the right mate,
but through being the right mate.

~ Barnett R. Brickner

Changes to the Marital-Family System

We've established that the career-to-home transition affects us personally, but how does it affect our marriage? Consider a baby mobile. When we move one arm of the mobile, we see that the remainder of the parts respond as well, some more energetically than others. A similar cause-and-effect occurs with the family. If we make a change to one member of the family, the rest must also adjust accordingly, though not all necessarily to the same degree.

But before we discuss the ways the career transition may affect our marriage, we need to step back and examine the impact children have on marriage in general. The discouraging news is that having children generally decreases marital satisfaction. Psychology professors Philip and Carolyn Cowan of the University of California studied this issue and found: "A surprisingly high proportion of couples experience increased tension, conflict, distress and divorce in the early years after arrival of the first child."

Diane Sollee, director of the Coalition for Marriage, Family, and Couples Education, summarized it this way in a 2004 article in *USA Today*: "The public doesn't realize at all that the birth of the first baby is the biggest challenge of marriage."

We need to be prepared for the strain on our marriage that a new baby creates, particularly during the early years. For those who already have children, this is stating the obvious. But for other mothers-to-be also pondering sacrificing their career to stay home, you're likely wondering if the lack of income will compound the strain. The good news is that having less money doesn't necessarily equate to a less happy marriage. Researchers at San Diego State University, the University of Georgia, and the U.S. Air Force Academy, analyzed data from 148 studies on marital contentment. They discovered that when wealthier couples had children, they suffered a drop in marital satisfaction much higher than that experienced by middle- or low-income parents.

But could the loss of income at the same time that you are bringing home a baby really help to *improve* your marriage? Let's be honest. The sudden drop in income is likely to be a stressor in the short term. But in the long run, you could find yourself less sidetracked by the trappings that significant income can create and focused more on the intangible aspects of your marriage and family that money simply can't buy.

Transforming Roles

As we transition from career to home, we shift from a more contemporary marriage arrangement to one that is more traditional. But, while most of us are happy to spend more time with our children, we generally aren't that excited about taking on a larger share of the chores. While it is true that the parent at home can be expected to do the bulk of the housework, some husbands may feel that all of the work is the responsibility of the stay-at-home mom. Carolyn, a middle school counselor and mother of three, was stung when her husband revealed his mindset: "He made the mistake once of saying that he 'works all week, so sweeping the floor was my job.' I was so upset that I was speechless. I've never been speechless. I just took a deep breath and calmly asked him if he really meant to hurt me by saying that. He quickly apologized."

But while most couples eventually adjust to the change, some of us may feel that a few kinks remain to be worked out. Kimberly, a teacher and a mother of two, explains:

> Now that I am at home, my husband expects me to handle
> pretty much everything, from the kids to all the needs of the
> house. The only tasks he still considers his are mowing the
> lawn and cleaning the garage (his sanctuary). I guess I should
> be willing to accept that because he works all day and takes
> care of the finances. But there are times when I think his
> expectations are a little too much.

Joycelyn, a communication specialist and mother of two, has also experienced frustration during the transformation of roles:

> Before we had children, my husband and I split the cooking
> and laundry. I did the rest of the indoor chores, and he took
> care of most of the ones outdoors. I now do the cooking and
> laundry almost exclusively. While I agree this is probably fair
> since I only work part time, I resent it sometimes. I feel like
> a maid. Before we had children, we went to the grocery store
> together, and he helped make food decisions. Now I get no
> input for meals, only scowls when my husband doesn't like
> what we're having for dinner. (And, yes, I do politely tell him
> where to stick it when he does this.)

Katrina, teacher and a mother of three, has also experienced some feelings of resentment regarding the change:

> *My husband goes to work, has a task or two for the day, eats*
> *a gourmet lunch, then finishes his task. He accomplishes*
> *something tangible that he can see. On the other hand, my*
> *work is never finished. I know that I have worked all day, but*
> *I just can't see the results. My kids are smiling, they are fed,*
> *they are clothed and clean, but I look at the mountains of toys,*
> *the kitchen that seems to be open at all times of the day, and*
> *I can't see progress. As a stay-at-home parent, you have to*
> *accept that a choice was provided and a choice was made.*
> *You have chosen to do this. I had to accept that my house*
> *would come second to my kids. My husband, on the other*
> *hand, had to come to the realization that, yes, this is work, and,*
> *no, I wasn't sitting around watching soap operas all day. (I left*
> *him home for a weekend once, and he finally got it.)*

This marital adjustment can, indeed, take some getting used to, but the good news is that most couples eventually discover that the arrangement works well. Kimberly, our teacher, explains: "My family, especially my husband, loves the fact that I am home. When I talk about going back to work, he starts to question why and gives me reasons why I am needed at home. Our marriage is wonderful. The roles are now better defined."

Michelle, veterinarian and mother of three, says this about the change: "Since I've come home, I think my husband feels more like a man. He's become more of a person I can lean on. He treats me more tenderly and gently, more like a woman. He appears to have more confidence, too. It's definitely been a positive move for both my husband and the children."

The Big Four: Chores, Finances, Parenting, and Power

Four major debates are universal to all marriages, and all are affected in some way by the career-to-home transition.

Chores—A study at the University of California at Berkeley tracked 100 couples from their first pregnancy through their child's entry into kindergarten and found that the primary source of conflict during the first three years of parenthood involved the division of labor.

One day, I was complaining to a friend about the impossible amount of housework in my home, and she asked, "Does your husband show appreciation for all you do?" I gave this some thought and said, "Yeah, I guess, but I'm not sure it matters."

You see, the nature of housework is so unchallenging and so uninspiring that I could hardly take a compliment as anything more than a joke. I mean, what could he say that would help? "Gosh, babe, that countertop looks so spectacular, you'd think the sparkle fairy cleaned it!" Or maybe he could give me a wink and say, "Gee, honey, I really like the aesthetically pleasing way you stacked those dishes in the dishwasher. Did you experiment with a different loading technique today?" If he was feeling particularly sentimental one evening, he might call me to his side, look tenderly into my eyes, and say, "I just wanted you to know that I sense your love for me in the way you fold my underwear."

The way Tim shows appreciation is to help me when he comes home. That simple act conveys the message that he recognizes that I am not the maid and that I, too, work. Now, don't get me wrong. The division of labor should be fair. If your husband is hard at work all day, you can't reasonably expect him to come home and do two or three more hours of nonstop housework every evening. But getting even a little help at the end of a long day is grand. .

So how do we get our man to help? Sex, of course. Next time you are slaving over the kitchen sink, unbutton your blouse a couple of notches and purr:

> "Baby, have you heard about the research coming out of the Love Lab of Dr. John Gottman of the University of Washington? Seems when men help more around the house, their wives are more likely to get in the mooooood." At this point, you should whip your hair back in a hot, sexy manner (being careful not to hurt your back), rock your hips over to where he's sitting, then whisper in his ear, "I just thought you might really want to know." Don't forget to wink over your shoulder as you walk away towards the bedroom.

Clearly, when our husbands help us around the house, we can interpret that as a sign of love, which, in turn, helps us to find them more attractive. But here's the catch: When our husbands help, they typically want to know that their work is appreciated. While we are likely to see their contribution as a natural part of their marital duty, they are more likely to see it as a special favor they're doing for us. This can be a tough concept for liberated women like us to accept. But you'll need to get past it in a hurry if you are seriously looking for more help. So stop nagging. Instead, on those occasions when you catch your husband cleaning, give him a big hug, a pinch on the rear, or a sultry wink-wink. It will help assure that he cleans again.

Now what should you do if you happen to have a husband who never cleans? Walk up to him, give him an incredibly juicy lip lock and thank him for doing the dishes. When he confesses that he actually never did the dishes, look surprised. Say, "Oh," and walk away, forgoing the over-the-shoulder wink. He might get off his duff and work a little harder for that next kiss.

But if you've tried everything, with no results, look on the bright side by considering what our working sisters are dealing with. While the gender gap in family duties is narrowing, women continue to carry the bulk of the workload in dual-income families. A Labor Department-sponsored time-use survey, conducted by the U.S. Census Bureau, found that employed women averaged one more hour per day of housework than did employed men. The survey also found that women spent an average of 2.7 hours caring for their children per day, compared to 1.2 hours for men.

Sometimes the change in roles can take on an interesting twist. Jenny, a teacher and a mother of five, had an unusual problem many of us would envy:

> *When we were first married, my husband did all the cooking*
> *and grocery shopping. When we had our second baby, I*
> *transitioned to stay-at-home. I began thinking that I should*
> *learn how to cook and do the grocery shopping because I*
> *was home now. It was really a challenge at first because my*
> *husband felt like I was moving in on his turf, whereas I felt*
> *like I was just helping him out and he didn't appreciate it.*
> *After a short period of weirdness, the situation smoothed*
> *itself out. Now, we plan our menu together for the week. I do*
> *the grocery shopping most of the time. We both share in the*
> *cooking. Some meals he cooks; some meals I cook. Whoever*
> *cooks, the other cleans up!*

Jenny is correct in stressing that most of our adjustments eventually settle out. In the meantime, it helps to sit down with your spouse and agree on a plan to divide the chores. This reduces the chances for misunderstanding and its odds-on progeny, resentment. Remember, too, that the duties will need to be readjusted as your children grow and your family changes.

If the chores are bringing you down or causing friction in your marriage, consider hiring occasional help if you are able to afford it. I've actually witnessed career mothers criticize stay-at-home moms for hiring cleaners, as if dual-income families were the only ones entitled to this privilege. With the draft of this book due and four young children on break, I absolutely had to hire someone to give me a hand this summer.

After 10 years at home, I don't care what people think anymore. Cleaning sucks. If I want to spend my money on a housekeeper and skip the Visa payment, that's my business. Chores are neverending drudgery. They depress me. To have someone come by every two weeks to scrub toilets allows me to spend more time with my family and my writing. Money well spent.

Finances—Money is another source of friction. The sudden and dramatic loss of your income, combined with the endless onslaught of bills and the ever increasing costs associated with growing children, all exacerbate the situation. Financial problems cause stress, which inevitably leads to arguments.

Your husband may now be the breadwinner, but that doesn't necessarily imply that he should be in charge of the money. Regardless of who brings home the bacon, the person who is the better money manager should take primary responsibility for maintaining the budget and paying the bills.

In our home, Tim manages the money because, well, I'm irresponsible. But just because I'm no Warren Buffet doesn't mean that I don't make out. Tim transfers a fixed chunk of every paycheck into my checking account, with which I am entrusted to buy food, clothing, household incidentals, and other immediate needs. I don't raid the primary bank accounts, which Tim manages, without first getting the green light. The money in those accounts is used to pay the mortgage, insurance, utilities, charities, and loans. We've experimented with other arrangements as well, but we've found that keeping our money separated in this manner reduces conflict by setting clearly defined responsibilities while providing each of us some autonomy in spending. Of course, this approach only works when the allowance budgeted is sufficient to cover costs. That's an entirely different subject…

If you find you are repeatedly at odds with your husband over money, be sure that both of you fully understand your financial situation and the amount of income required to pay the bills and meet your family's longer-term financial objectives. Doing this will help eliminate distrust and misunderstanding related to earnings and spending.

You also may want to step back and examine your individual belief systems. What does money mean to each of you? Some see money as a way to enjoy life, to travel or play, so they tend to spend it now. Others see money as a form of security and want to tuck any extra dollars away. As both of you examine your personal relationship with money, it may help to understand the manner in which your parents managed their finances. By taking the time to appreciate why each of you might relate to money in the way you do, you strengthen your ability to empathize with each other's unique position. This understanding will form the foundation for reaching a suitable compromise.

Parenting—After the birth of your first child, you will discover immediately that parenting style is a subject ripe for disagreement. I honestly can't recall Tim and I ever having a serious argument before our children were born, but we sure did afterward. While arguments can be unsettling, they should be expected when you consider that you and your spouse are two unique individuals, arriving from different childhood experiences and coming together to raise a child.

Before the birth of our first child, Tim and I attended a parenting class together. We found it beneficial for introducing what, at the time, was a very foreign concept to us. Perhaps more important, the class served as an excellent jumping-off point for discussion while we worked through our expectations about our upcoming role as parents. We highly recommend that both you and your spouse attend such a class as well, before your baby arrives, while you both are still in a comparatively relaxed and rational state of mind!

If you don't have the time to take a class, then both you and your spouse should write down questions and concerns you might have about parenting and answer them together. How much parental involvement and assistance can you expect from each other? What are your beliefs regarding discipline? Who will get up in the middle of the night when the baby cries?

When you experience a conflict of ideas, again, take a minute to examine your own childhood and the roles your parents played. Was Dad fully engaged with the day-to-day activities? Did he come home from work, play with the kids, then help them with homework? Did your spouse's father go straight to the television set with a dry martini in hand? If so, you will probably have drastically different expectations from one another. Understanding your spouse's past will help you relate to your husband's perspective, and he to yours, when conflict inevitably arises.

When you both actively seek to empathize with each other's viewpoint, you'll become more skilled at doing so, and you'll find that the frequency and magnitude of conflict with your spouse grows less over time. At the same time, your ever improving relational skills will be quietly shoring up your marriage against the challenges that eventually will present themselves once your child becomes a teenager.

Power—Our career and income can give us a measure of power and influence in our marriage. So, once you've left your career for home, you may feel as though you've also lost some of your importance along with that last paycheck. You need not feel this way.

Yes, you've changed roles, from breadwinner to caregiver, but your importance within the marriage hasn't decreased. In fact, the opposite is true. Your value to the marriage has increased greatly. A mature husband understands that he is part of a system in which each of you plays a critical role and that your role is ultimately beneficial to him.

Because you are at home, your husband is able to go to work each day with the freedom to concentrate more fully on his job. The potential benefits are not merely conjecture, as it has been shown that our service has tangible value outside the home as well. Results from the Institute for Social and Economic Research in the United Kingdom found that husbands with wives at home enjoy more success in the workplace and earn higher wages. Your efforts at home may benefit your husband's health as well. Sociologists Vincent Duindam and Ed Spruijt of the Netherlands' Utrecht University found that the more hours a mother works outside the home, the poorer the fathers' physical and mental well-being.

Don't underestimate your importance in the relationship. Your husband relies heavily on you, just as you rely on him.

Communication

Some women notice a change in communication with their spouse after they've left their career. It can be helpful to study this type of change using the classic self-help reference, *I'm OK—You're OK*. In his bestselling book, Dr. Thomas A. Harris explores the three states of communication from Eric Berne's transactional analysis theory: Parent, Adult, and Child. As you might guess, the Parent state of communication is exemplified by the mantras we often heard from our own parents when we were children: "Chew with your mouth closed," "Wear your coat when you go outside," and so on. The Child state of communication reflects feelings and creativity, but is usually submissive and often inept. Finally, we have the Adult state, which is used to mediate between the Parent and Child states, acting very much like a computer that processes information logically. All of us shift among these three states throughout the day, so a number of different forms of interaction can result.

Let's apply the theory here. When we entered into marriage, many of us came in as equal partners with our spouses. We both had careers, we both brought in income, and, more than likely, there was an equitable division of domestic duties. As equal partners, many of us preferred our interactions to be on a more adult-to-adult level of communication.

But sometimes, the career-to-home transition changes the way we communicate with one another. For example, a husband may be more inclined to take on a parental role and begin speaking to his wife as if she is a child. Margie, a paralegal and mother of three, describes how the dynamics changed in her marriage after she left her career:

> For the first two years of our marriage, I pretty much
> supported my husband financially while he finished school. He
> often felt inadequate because of this. So, after I quit work and
> he began paying all of the bills, I guess he felt more compelled
> to "flex his muscles." He became more forthcoming with his
> criticisms. He often talked to me like he talked to the children.
> As you can imagine, it infuriated me and caused a lot of

friction. I thought, "How dare you talk to me like I am anything less that an equal partner in this marriage!"

A Parent-Child form of interaction between husband and wife isn't always negative. In fact, it can be quite the opposite. Let's say you've had a very rough day. Your husband recognizes this and gives you a back rub, makes a nice meal, and puts the kids to bed. Your spouse has assumed the Parent role while you are in a Child role. This interaction would be considered complimentary. But if, instead, he expected you to pull yourself up by your bootstraps and rationally handle your rough day like an adult, the transaction would be considered "crossed," meaning that you were looking for a nurturing Parent interaction but were met instead by the Adult. So we see that Parent-Child forms of interaction don't create problems; it is when communications are crossed that conflict can erupt.

Let's be clear. It can work to the disadvantage of the husband as well. For example, a mother might feel that only she is capable of being the home and child "expert." She may become quite critical of her husband when he attempts to care for their children or help around the house. She has assumed a parental state. This leaves her spouse with one of two choices. Either he can fulfill the role as incompetent father (by assuming the Child state), or he can resist her attempts to make him feel like a child. If he chooses the latter, conflict is likely to ensue.

It's good practice in conflict resolution to keep the focus on the specific problem and how it affects you. If your husband frequently assumes a parental role in his communication with you, say something like, "When you speak to me that way, it makes me feel like a child." Be consistent. Eventually your spouse will learn to catch himself before speaking to you in a parental manner, and reoccurrences of such behavior will decrease in frequency.

Of course, these suggestions do not apply if you or your husband has become verbally or physically abusive. Conflict on that level requires immediate professional intervention.

Improve Your Marriage

Understanding that your marriage will probably be under a great deal of stress as you adjust to new children and your changing roles, it is important that you invest the time to nurture your relationship with your spouse during this challenging period. Following are a few suggestions to help strengthen your marriage.

Avoid Comparisons—Resist the temptation to compare your spouse to others. There is no shortage of stories about how great other husbands are. The ensuing comparisons will only make you feel resentful or bitter. After years of counseling couples, I've learned firsthand that what you might see on the surface with others doesn't always reflect what you'd get with the whole package. You'd do better to focus on your husband's strengths rather than concentrate on his weaknesses.

Touch—This is an important form of communication in a marriage. Have you ever noticed how cold a relationship appears when couples seem unable to touch and hold each other? It's as if there is an invisible wall between them. Make it a point to hold each other. Take your husband's hand while walking at the mall; touch him on the shoulder as you walk by; greet him with a kiss and a hug—daily.

Flirt—Always look for opportunities to flirt with your spouse. Provocative greeting cards, occasional slaps on the rear, suggestive whispers, a wink from across the room—these all add dimension to a marriage and keep the passion alive. Tim and I like to send flirtatious e-mails to one another while Tim is at work. Is it a violation of corporate policy? Maybe. But that's all part of what makes it so exciting!

Play—Find an activity that you both enjoy and do it regularly. Tim and I date as often as finances permit. Lately, we've been exploring historic downtown Savannah together. Katrina and her husband put some spark back in their relationship by enrolling in dance classes. "We took ballroom and salsa dance lessons once a week for six months. At home, we would often practice our moves and put on a show for our kids. They loved it!"

A friend told me a story that involved her preteen children. In a misguided effort to put their children first, she and her husband had not gone on a date since the birth of their first child. Now, after almost a decade of self-abandonment, they decided they were ready to go out. Alone. They sat their children down to process their feelings. What was the result? Their children not only frowned on the idea, they ordered their parents to stay home. What did the parents do? They complied!

Our children need to understand that a healthy marriage is a vital element of a healthy family. This marital relationship began before they came into the world and will continue long after they leave home. So, while we are willing to make great sacrifices for our children, it will not be at the expense of our marriage.

Kids naturally think that the world revolves around them. Spending time alone with our spouse helps send the message to our children that they aren't the only ones in the family. Dating makes it clear that Mom and Dad have their own special relationship and that they need time with each other occasionally to keep it healthy.

Make Love—Regular sex is essential to a good marriage. I once had a client who was experiencing marital problems. She said that she and her husband had been working through them, but progress was slow. I asked her when they had last had sex. "Over a year ago," was her reply! I explained to her that she was unlikely to make progress with her marriage while withholding sex at the same time. She apparently got the point because, at our next session, she said that she had reintroduced sex and that her relationship with her spouse was showing great improvement.

Withholding sex is a game too often played in marriage, one that can seriously damage relationships. Keep in mind that the opposite is generally true as well: increasing the frequency of making love usually improves a marriage.

Follow the Rules of Engagement—All marriages have conflict; it's a fact of life. But how we handle these conflicts can have a lasting impact on our marriage and on our physical well-being. Research at Ohio State University showed that when couples used sarcasm, insults, criticism, and put-downs during conflict, their bodies produced higher levels of stress hormones. Follow-up studies in subsequent years showed that those participants with higher stress hormones were likely to report greater declines in marital satisfaction and, ultimately, were more likely to be divorced.

Fight fair. Stay focused on the problem and don't use the argument as an opportunity to degrade or insult your spouse. When your goal is to hurt, routine arguments can cause long-term damage. The dirtier we fight, the worse it tends to be on the next occasion and the more difficult it becomes to repair.

When you become very angry, give yourself a chance to cool down before responding. Put yourself in your spouse's position and try to see the problem from his perspective. Be willing to compromise. Realize that some arguments have no apparent resolution.

And, finally, avoid relaying the more distasteful aspects of your husband's behavior to your friends or family. If you plan to be married for a very long time, it's simply a good habit to limit the number of people with whom you share your marital problems.

Give Each Other Space—Space can become a treasured commodity when you have children. Both husbands and wives need occasional time alone, particularly when the children are young. In a healthy marriage, giving your husband the space he needs will likely be a favor that he returns to you. I often barter with Tim for space. To have some time to myself, I offer to watch the kids at some other time so he, too, can have time alone. So, instead of two people both struggling to make progress amid the chaos of children, we take turns, assuring that we both have the uninterrupted time we occasionally need.

Along these same lines, resist the temptation to dump the baby in your husband's arms the minute he comes home from a long day at work. Give him a chance to unwind, change his clothes, and reacclimate. Then dump the baby in his arms!

Avoid Jealousy—When we accept our redefined role in the marriage, we need to understand that the perks associated with our new job also change, and that they will not be similar to those of our spouse. Tim has to do a fair amount of traveling for his job, and it's hard for me not to feel a twinge of envy when he calls home from a mountaintop in California or a pub in Berlin. Sometimes, just hearing about all the cool things he's accomplishing at work can make me jealous.

But those are just his perks. Most days, he has to wake up much earlier than I do, and he arrives home late in the evening. To go to the gym, he has to leave the house long before daylight. He rarely has time to make progress on the ever growing list of tasks at home. I, on the other hand, have the time to balance my checkbook, work out, or swim with my little ones at the pool. I'm able to use my son's nap time to write or read a book if I so choose. Sure, it's not Berlin, but these are some of the tangible perks of my job as an at-home mother.

It's easier to avoid jealousy when we take time to balance the benefits of being an at-home mother against the drawbacks. It is also helpful when we are able to empathize with the more undesirable aspects of our spouse's career.

Forgive, Forgive, and Forgive—The secret to a strong marriage isn't the perfect relationship or the perfect spouse, it's forgiveness. We all screw up, sometimes royally. Forgiveness means that we move forward, ignoring the inclination to revisit the past over and over again. If your marriage is suffering from some old grievance, and divorce is not an option, then you have nothing left but to forgive.

My Hope for Your Future

The arrival of a new baby and the loss of your career as you transition to home are very significant life events that will strain even the strongest union. Learn to recognize the dangers, obvious and subtle, that can jeopardize your marriage. Be proactive in taking steps to protect and build your relationship so your marriage will survive the many significant challenges ahead.

My wish for you and your spouse is that you will be wonderfully successful in your role as parents, that you will be refined and strengthened by the process, and that you will grow old gracefully, as best friends, finding deep and lasting contentment in each other's arms.

In a world in which marriage is so often an object of derision, may yours silence the critics.

CHAPTER 8

Depression

The world is full of people looking for
spectacular happiness while they snub
contentment.

~ Doug Larson

A Common Problem

Shortly after the birth of our third child, I had a routine appointment with my OB/GYN. Once again, I was a postpartum frazzled mess, a walking zombie, going through the motions of caring for my children. I was anxious, overwhelmed, and miserable. My goal was to find a way through each day so I could return to the refuge of sleep at night. Now, I found myself in front of my doctor, and I gave her an earful.

When I finished dumping all my complaints, she surprised me by suggesting I try an antidepressant, "Just until things get better." Insulted, I declined her offer. A couple of months later, I met with my primary physician. After describing an array of physical complaints, I was again offered antidepressants. I was indignant. How dare these doctors ignore my complaints and treat me like a mental patient!

Clearly, I was depressed, and that fact seemed obvious to everyone but me. Here I was, a therapist by trade, yet I was unable, or perhaps unwilling, to recognize the symptoms.

Maternal depression is extremely common. From 50 to 75 percent of all new mothers experience some form of emotional letdown following the birth of their children. Commonly referred to as the "baby blues," these symptoms often manifest themselves as anxiety, irritability, or crying spells. For most women, the symptoms are short-lived and eventually disappear on their own.

A more serious form of depression, called postpartum depression, afflicts 10 percent of all new mothers and can first reveal itself anywhere from days to an entire year after the baby is born. The symptoms of postpartum depression include:

- Depressed mood
- Poor appetite or eating too much
- Crying for no apparent reason
- Loss of interest in things that once brought pleasure
- Having thoughts of hurting oneself or the baby
- Feeling overwhelmed
- Anxiousness or irritability
- Psychomotor agitation or retardation
- Feeling emotionally numb
- Sleeping too much or suffering from insomnia
- Fatigue
- Low self-worth
- Lack of interest in sex
- Feeling of hopelessness
- Difficulty concentrating or making decisions

One of the reasons we might fail to identify the symptoms of postpartum depression is that it can have characteristics similar to those of normal postpartum exhaustion. This may be why I failed to recognize it in myself. Although experts are not entirely sure what causes postpartum depression, most believe it may have biological roots in the sudden drop in estrogen, progesterone, and thyroid hormones after birth. The dramatic life changes that occur after the birth of a child are also certainly contributors, especially for those mothers who have left their careers at roughly the same time as giving birth.

Another very serious disorder can occur during this time. Postpartum psychosis afflicts about 1 in 1,000 new mothers and usually appears suddenly within the first few weeks after delivery. Symptoms include:

- EXTREME AGITATION
- INSOMNIA
- DELUSIONS
- HALLUCINATIONS
- SUICIDAL OR HOMICIDAL THOUGHTS
- ODD BEHAVIORS OR FEELINGS

If you believe you may be suffering from postpartum depression or psychosis, it is critical that you call your doctor immediately, even before you turn this page. Explain your symptoms and ask to be seen right away. A relatively simple salivary test can be performed to check your hormone levels. Your doctor will also be able to determine if other medical conditions might be causing your symptoms. These conditions could include anemia, hypoglycemia, sleep apnea, low adrenal function, or postpartum thyroiditis.

While some doctors are comfortable prescribing medications for the mind (psychotropics), others may refer you to a psychiatrist. Because psychiatrists specialize in the medical treatment of disorders influencing the mind, I encourage you to see a psychiatrist, as opposed to a general practitioner or OB/GYN, for any psychotropic medication requirements.

Psychiatrists will see that you receive a complete psychological assessment, work with you to find the right medication to reduce your symptoms, monitor for side effects, and stay alert to any sudden changes in your symptoms.

Most psychiatrists today perform very little psychotherapy (talk therapy) and, instead, focus their energies on medical intervention. If you feel that you would benefit from psychotherapy, ask for a referral to a therapist or psychologist, preferably someone who specializes in postpartum disorders.

Postpartum support groups can also be helpful. Usually facilitated by a professional therapist, such groups offer a supportive place where women can discuss their concerns with others who are experiencing similar issues. Contact your local hospital for information on postpartum groups.

Lessons from Andrea Yates

Andrea Yates was a nurse, turned stay-at-home mother, who, in 2001, drowned her five young children in a bathtub. The tragedy received widespread media scrutiny and brought to national attention the very real dangers of severe depression. While this case is extreme, it does illustrate two important points.

The first, and perhaps most obvious, point is that postpartum depression and psychosis must always be taken seriously. Andrea Yates's actions suggest the need for all of us to be mindful of the state of our mental health and to seek help when we need it. Proper treatment for depression is the medical equivalent of taking insulin for diabetes. Don't be ashamed if you're experiencing a psychological issue; just take care of it. And keep in mind that, although you may be having problems with depression now, it doesn't mean that you will indefinitely. I have known many friends and clients who've benefited from antidepressants that were prescribed for just a short period until their hormones, or the craziness of their lives, settled down.

The second point is that we need to accept our limitations. Andrea Yates had a history of mental illness, with several previous periods of treatment for depression and psychosis. In addition to being the mother of five children, she home-schooled her children. I know a woman who has home-schooled nine children and did it well, so I want to be clear that this isn't about home-schooling, but rather about adding stress to instability. In the Yates case, we have a woman suffering from a severe form of mental illness, with five young children whom she is also trying to educate. Compounding the enormous stress was the fact that her father was ill and dying. Andrea Yates's disability was either ignored or not recognized, making all ingredients present for a mental health disaster.

I have said this before and I'm going to say it again. The parenting gig is nothing like the work gig. Sure, work can be stressful; but it pales in comparison to the stress of raising kids. Don't fall into the trap of believing that you have to be the same superhero at home that you were at the office. At the office, you could take control decisively and move things forward. With children, there is far less predictability, creating an environment in which we often have less control.

Before you add one more thing to your plate, honestly assess where you are, not where you think you should be. I personally know that I would be emotionally and psychologically unable to deal with home-schooling my children at this stage in their lives. I can't manage any more pets. My ability to work part time is limited. I am unable to volunteer for many activities right now. And, as much as we love our children, it is clear that having a fifth baby at this time would probably send my husband and me over the edge! While it can be hard for me to accept that I am no longer the superhero of my past, I am now more honest about my limitations and what I can handle outside of my world of four children.

Recognizing Depression

Most of us will not face depression as severe and long-lasting as that experienced by Andrea Yates. But that doesn't mean we can't, on occasion, encounter a very rough bout. Tammy, a quality assurance auditor and mother of two, shares her experience:

> When my daughter was two years old, I went into counseling after a particularly bad episode of depression. One day, I was heading east on the 10 freeway, and I wondered how far I could get before my husband missed me. The urge to keep driving was almost too much. I had never been so sad. At the time, I didn't relate it to hormones. I just thought I was mourning the loss of the life I had—traveling, throwing parties, going out with my husband, sleeping in, taking naps. I felt so selfish. My baby was probably nine months old before I could say I loved her. I think it took me 18 months to really bond with her. It was terrible. Sometimes, I would just look at her and cry. I never felt like I would hurt my baby or myself, but what scared me is that I didn't really feel anything toward her, one way or the other.

Old Pain Resurfacing—While environmental and hormonal changes certainly may contribute to your depression, there is also the possibility that your depression was always there, hidden beneath your exciting career. A flight into work is a wonderful way to keep depression at bay. By staying busy, we don't have the time to deal with what is really bothering us. Whether old pains from childhood, self-loathing, or anger, for the first time in perhaps a long while, we can now actually hear ourselves think. Deeply repressed depression may suddenly float to the surface.

If it appears that old issues are, indeed, resurfacing, it would behoove you to seek counseling. You may even be able to find a support group that addresses your particular issue. Instead of looking for another way to cloak your pain, consider this an opportunity to face what's truly bothering you and conquer it.

Coping with Depression

If your depression is severe or if psychosis is present, seek medical treatment. Your doctor will determine if there are any physical causes for your depression and will give you an objective opinion on the severity of your symptoms. If your depression is mild, however, self-help techniques may be all that you need to feel well again.

Cognitive Strategies—If you came to me for therapy, seeking help for depression, I would first examine how your thought processes might be feeding your problem. People who are depressed tend to be overly self-critical, have unrealistic expectations, engage in negative self-talk, magnify their failures, and dwell on negative feedback. This said, I would use the following thought-altering strategies to raise your mood.

Examine Irrational Thought Patterns—Happy people think happy thoughts. If you're in the habit of seeing the glass as half-empty, this could be the root of your problem. To change habitual thought patterns, we first need to identify irrational or distorted thoughts and then replace them with those that are rational. Here are some examples of how this is done:

Irrational—"No one appreciates me."
Rational—"Although I sometimes feel unappreciated, my work is of value and appreciated."

Irrational—"My children are out of control."
Rational—"All children can be trying at times."

Irrational—"We will not survive financially."
Rational—"Although we are going through a difficult time, we can be proactive and make this work."

Irrational—"I am wasting my life."
Rational—"My life is an investment in the future."

Irrational—"I have ruined my career."
Rational—"While there will be consequences for my decision, most women do not have a problem returning to work after being home."

Irrational—"I don't have any friends."
Rational—"It can take time to make new friends. I will put myself in places that will increase the probability that I will meet them."

Irrational—"My home is so dirty, it will eventually be condemned."
Rational—"If my house is condemned, it will be a good thing because I won't have to clean it anymore. Besides, a clean house is a sign of a boring woman."

Irrational—"My workday never ends."
Rational—"Oh wait, that was rational. My workday never does end!"

Pay attention to your own thoughts. Say them out loud if it helps. Are they repeatedly negative and demoralizing? If so, learn to replace thoughts that are irrational with those that are rational, even humorous, as they occur.

Reframe Events—We live in a neighborhood where many children run about much of the day. The kids can often be found playing in the driveway in front of our house. Because the garage contains the typical array of dangerous items—shovels, tools, mowers, paint—Tim decided to follow the lead of our other neighbors by asking the neighborhood children to stay out of the garage.

My son James tried to explain the new rule to a neighbor boy one day. The boy looked perplexed and replied, "Well, I know why we don't let kids in our garage. We have two expensive cars. But I don't know why kids can't go in your garage. All you have is a dirty van with a big piece of gum on it."

That just about summed it up. We did have a dirty van with a huge piece of gum on the side of it. The gum had been on the car for months. Nobody knew where it came from. Every day I'd stare at it, but for some reason, I just couldn't muster the emotional energy needed to deal with it. It was gross. It disturbed me. And there it sat. But something changed in the way I looked at it once my son told me this story. We both started laughing. The gum didn't change, but how I perceived it did. The gum went from disturbing to hilarious in a matter of seconds, and I was finally able to scrape it off.

Let Go of Perfectionism—Are you trying to be too perfect? Does your house have to be spotless, your children clean, your hair just right? Maybe these expectations are making you a little nutty.

I attended a birthday party for a friend of my daughter's who was turning four. At the time, my Maria was enrolled in a very popular part-time preschool program. I couldn't help but notice that each party Maria was invited to that year was growing increasingly fabulous.

And this one was by far the best. The party was on the birthday girl's front lawn. Mom had perfectly decorated each table with fresh flowers that coordinated with the tablecloths. Lunch featured a light chicken salad served on fresh croissants, along with a delicious green salad topped with walnuts, blue cheese, and mandarin oranges, all served with sweet tea. The cake, a work of art, was homemade.

The mother planned several craft projects for the girls to enjoy, including painting flowerpots and decorating garden hats. Oh, and don't forget the games! It had to be the best birthday party for a little girl ever, and I'm guessing it must have cost Mom several hundred dollars to pull it off.

But the therapist in me, the same person whose daughter had a birthday following hot on the heels of this incredible event, kept an eye on the unraveled mother. She wasn't able to smile, and she repeatedly barked at her kids and husband. While she was successful in hosting the best little girl birthday party ever, she had also inadvertently turned herself into a stressed-out bitch.

Needless to say, Maria had her birthday party that year in the gymnasium at the YMCA. Kroger decorated her cake, and Domino's delivered the pizza. And you know what? Maria didn't notice that she didn't have the best little girl birthday party ever. She was having too much fun. And so was her mom.

Linda, a jury administrator and mother of three, illustrates the proper method for taking the business of housekeeping a little less seriously: "After knocking myself out cleaning every day, and nobody really noticing, I decided to cut corners instead by just straightening things up and spraying a little Febreze in the air so that it smelled like I had been hard at work all day. It really helped to free up some of my time!"

Sure, it might sound like a cruel trick, but trust me. Whatever Linda's husband loses in cleanliness returns to him many times over in a happier wife.

Learn to Accept What Is—The dance of the stay-at-home mother is composed of three steps forward and two steps back. Whether it's permanent marker on the newly hung wallpaper or vomit on the couch, this two-step can be disheartening. But when our expectations for our lives look more like those of the young mothers on the glossy cover of *Parenting* magazine, and our reality is closer to an episode of *The Simpsons*, the dissonance eventually leads to depression. The reality is, our kids are going to trash our home, and, despite thousands of dollars in skin care products, we will inevitably age and play the part. What's happening to us is happening in every home with children, in every part of the world. What makes you think your home should be the exception?

If there is a great chasm between how your life is and the way you think it should be, you will be unhappy. Practice letting go. Dwelling on the many everyday problems of your life, your failures, or your weaknesses will only make you bitter and discontented. Donna, a design engineer and mother of two, applies this mind-set to the reality we can all relate to—growing older:

> When I was young, I thought that physical beauty was very important. Not that I was beautiful. Far from it. But I always wanted to be. Now that I am older and a mother, I have a different perspective on the whole thing. Occasionally, I'll pass by a mirror and see gray roots that need touch-up or one neglected Cro-Magnon eyebrow sticking out, and I'll say to myself,

"Thank God my self-esteem wasn't built on my looks!" Self-esteem comes from self-approval. I need to be able to look in the mirror and see a person who approves of her life. Ninety-nine out of one hundred days I do. And on the one hundredth day, I color my hair and pluck my Cro-Magnon eyebrow.

The Grass Isn't Always Greener—It may seem like the women who continue to work have it better than we do, but their life is certainly no picnic either. I knew a woman whose daughter would get carsick and vomit every single morning on their way to day care. Career mothers are often up till the wee hours of the morning, folding laundry and balancing their checkbook. That's certainly not my idea of a glamorous life. The grass may indeed look greener because they can afford more expensive fertilizer, but trust me, they're doing a lot of mowing.

Instead of focusing on your problems, focus on your blessings. While career mothers are running out the door at 6:30 in the morning, you're just starting your first cup of coffee. While other moms are racing down the road with a steering wheel in one hand and a breast pump in the other, you're still sitting in your rocker singing to your baby. And, best of all, you can go shopping during the day when there aren't any crowds at the mall!

Action Strategies

You've explored some of the underlying thought processes that can contribute to depression. But once you've let go of the root causes, what steps can you take to help maintain a positive mood? Consider the following action strategies.

Get a Life—Some women have taken the concept of being a stay-at-home mother to the extreme. Being at home does not preclude you from having a life. To stay balanced, mothers need to have borders beyond caring for their children. It's fairly easy to spot a stay-at-home mother who is off-balance: she is usually miserable, angry, and obsessive in matters pertaining to her children.

A career mother and friend called me the other night to tell me of an experience she had with a stay-at-home mother. She had attended Parents' Night at her son's school where there was a parent-volunteer sign-up sheet. My friend waited behind a woman at the sign-up table who, in a martyred voice, complained that it appeared she would have to, once again, be the "room mother," because all the other mothers of the students in the class worked. My friend, not immediately realizing that she was about to become a player in this woman's game, happily offered to take the job and put her name on the sign-up sheet.

Her reign was short lived, however, as the very next day she received a call from the classroom teacher asking her to resign her post. Apparently, the martyred stay-at-home mother had called the teacher, concerned that my working friend would not have the time to fulfill her duties as classroom mom. She recommended the teacher find someone else to fill the position.

In this case, the martyr couldn't fathom the thought of anything good coming from outside her at-home world. By purposely sabotaging the efforts of the career mother, the at-home martyr provided ample evidence that she needed to broaden her world, and, basically, get a life.

Volunteer—If you need to expand your world, consider volunteering. Numerous studies have shown that volunteering can improve well-being, happiness, self-esteem, and physical health. Volunteering forces us to break away from our personal pity party and discover greater meaning in life. Ashley, a district sales manager and mother of two, immersed herself in civic activities after she started staying home: "I went from traveling for a living in sales to being immediately grounded with kids. I had a very difficult time 'always being around,' so I joined the board of a local art museum. It keeps me busy and helps me to feel that I am a part of something important."

What would be fulfilling for you? How about helping out at a wildlife preserve or pet shelter? Perhaps you'd like to be more involved with your church? Is there a community project in your area that could use some help? Or maybe you might get a kick out of helping a local politician win office. The possibilities are unlimited.

I've decided that I am not the homeroom mother type, but I do enjoy giving presentations at my children's school. I've talked to the students about a number of subjects, from long-distance backpacking and the science of food dehydration to my home state of Hawaii. I've taught the kids about volcanoes, Hawaiian history, and even hula dancing. When I visit the school today, students still remember me as the "hula lady!"

Make Friends—Sometimes leaving a career also means leaving behind friends. Don't minimize the importance of friends; they can be your lifeline during this time. Besides being someone to talk to, a friend can be your partner in survival. I've made great friends over the years during some very difficult stages with my kids. We've taken care of each other's children, made meals for each other, and even helped the other clean before company arrived. Friends were crucial for Jackie when she left her career as an office manager to be home with her new twins:

> After my twins were born, they spent their first two weeks in
> the intensive care unit. I never talked to anyone about how
> scared, depressed, sad, and lonely I was really feeling. Not even
> to my husband. At night, I would hide under my covers. I would
> get nervous thinking about how I was going to handle the
> next morning with my babies. Fortunately, I found a group of
> women through a local hospital who all had twins around the
> same time that I did. Every Monday, we would pack up our

kids and go to a home of someone in the group. We all loved our time together and stayed as long as our babies could hold out. Thank God for my girlfriends!

Look for new friends during special events at your child's school and at playgrounds, churches, classes, gyms, museums, libraries, and community swimming pools. If you meet somebody who interests you, don't just say goodbye and walk away. Get her phone number or e-mail address and make plans to get together.

I've also met some of my friends online. There is obviously an element of danger in doing this, and you must exercise discernment. But with due caution, you can get to know great people via Web sites and bulletin boards and through e-mail. Tim and I became friends with a couple from Canada over the Internet through our shared interest in backpacking foods and the outdoors. Two years ago, we took our children with us to Ontario, where we joined our Canadian acquaintances for a week-long canoe outing in the Algonquin Wilderness. Even though we had never met them face-to-face before the trip, we had become well acquainted through many phone calls and e-mails. We ultimately enjoyed a wonderful adventure together that we'll never forget.

You may also want to consider joining one of the many support groups available to moms such as Mothers of Preschoolers (MOPS) or the International Moms Club. If there are no groups in your local area, you might want to use your entrepreneurial skills to start your own.

Keep a Journal—Journaling can be an excellent way to vent your emotions. Research by James Pennebaker of the University of Texas at Austin found that writing about personal experiences in an emotional way for as little as 15 minutes for a period of three days brings about improvements in physical and mental health.

Journaling can be effective at helping us to clarify our thoughts and feelings, understand ourselves better, find our own resolution to problems, reduce conflict with others, or simply de-stress. While I don't use a journal in the traditional sense, I frequently find myself using e-mail as a way to vent my feelings to my friends and family. Sometimes I don't even send the e-mails I've written. I find that just putting down my thoughts in writing can provide tremendous relief.

Taking Care of Your Body

Nutrition—This is not a good time to start a coffee and donut diet. Poor food choices, stress, nutritional deficiencies, drug use, and food allergies can all contribute to depression. In their 2004 book, *Prescription for Natural Cures*, James Balch and Mark Stengler recommend a diet rich in beans, nuts, seeds, lean poultry, eggs, and coldwater fish, along with reduced sugar intake, to combat depression. Supplements should include a high-potency multivitamin containing a B-complex. There are also several over-the-counter nutritional supplements reported to improve mood, including 5-hydrozytryptophan (5-HTP), Saint John's wort, and S-adenosylmethionine (SAMe). SAMe has been tested extensively in Europe as a mood enhancer and has been prescribed by doctors in many countries outside the United States for more than two decades. It is widely available over the counter. Tim and I take SAMe periodically, and we have both found that it does seem to significantly improve mood and reduce tension.

Always talk to your physician before taking any of these types of supplements. It is especially important to note that mood-enhancing supplements should not be consumed if you are already taking a prescription anti-depressant!

Exercise—*The British Journal of Sports Medicine* reported that aerobic exercise may work faster than medications to relieve depression. Twelve people with severe depression, 10 of whom had taken antidepressants with no improvement, exercised on a treadmill for 30 minutes each day. After 10 days, six of the patients were substantially less depressed, two were slightly less depressed, and four remained the same. Five of those who had tried antidepressant medications without success reported feeling substantially better.

Duke University Medical Center studied 156 elderly patients diagnosed with major depressive disorder and assigned them to three groups: exercise therapy, medication therapy, or a combination of both. After 16 weeks, researchers found that all three groups showed statistically significant improvement in their depression measurements. The research reported significant relief in 60.4 percent of the patients who exercised only, 65.5 percent of those who took medication only, and 68.8 percent in the combination group. Lead researcher James Blumenthal summarized the findings: "One of the conclusions we can draw from this is that exercise may be just as effective as medication and may be a better alternative for certain patients."

Mommy Time—Some days can be so difficult that we may find ourselves watching the clock until our husbands get home. Some of us may have the added stress of a spouse who travels often or is gone for months at a time, serving our country overseas.

We all need time away from our children, but it's not always easy to find and it can take some ingenuity to pull off. Consider putting your child to bed a little earlier than normal to enjoy some quiet time with your husband. Or how about arising before your children so you can enjoy a cup of coffee or put your makeup on in peace? Share a babysitter with a friend to reduce the cost of child care or take turns watching each other's kids on a regular basis so you can be assured of a break. Instead of always using your child's nap time to clean, take an occasional hot bath instead, read a novel, or catch a quick nap yourself. Even a few hours to yourself every week can rejuvenate your spirit and give you something to look forward to.

If your husband is in the military, contact the family services department and find out what resources are available to family members. Get together with other military wives to create a community of support and avoid isolating yourself.

Superwomen Still Get Depressed!

Many of us superwoman types may feel the need to hide our depression as if it were an indication of weakness or failure. The reality is that many of us do experience maternal depression, yet we may be too embarrassed to admit it. I find it encouraging that the topic is starting to receive increased attention as more accomplished women come forward to tell their story.

Actress Courteney Cox recently described having experienced postpartum depression. She told *USA Today*, "I went through a really hard time—not right after the baby, but when [Coco] turned six months. I couldn't sleep. My heart was racing. And I got really depressed. I went to the doctor and found out my hormones had been pummeled." Cox went on to discover that good friends and progesterone therapy helped to alleviate her postpartum depression.

If you were to perform a quick online search, you would discover the names of dozens of well-known people who've accomplished amazing things in their lives despite having struggled with some form of mental issue.

Among them are scientists, entertainers, artists, athletes, psychiatrists, Nobel Prize winners, composers, poets, authors, even leaders of countries.

Once we realize just how many famous people in history have struggled with mental illness, we realize that depression is not a sign of weakness but a challenge that we, too, can face and overcome. In fact, it is so often seen in great individuals that it may, indeed, be the catalyst feeding the rare passion that powers incredible achievement.

If you are experiencing maternal depression, be proactive and find the help you need. Don't let shame or pride keep you from achieving great things, too.

CHAPTER 9

Stay-at-Home Stress

*I was doing the family grocery shopping
accompanied by two children,
an event I hope to see included in the
Olympics in the near future.*

~ Anna Quindlen

Background to Stress

"T.G.I.M."—Thank God it's Monday!—was the expression used by Susan Kane, working mother and editor of *BabyTalk* magazine, as she went on to describe the previous weekend:

> When one kid wasn't crying or whining, the other one was.
> When one wasn't wrecking the house, the other one was. At
> one point, Nick was on a play date, and I'd just put Darcy
> down for a nap. At last, I thought, I can have a bit of peace.
> But I came downstairs from the nursery to a scene of such do-
> mestic chaos that my heart sank to my toes. The dining room
> was groaning under mountains of mail, catalogs, and lonely
> socks. The kitchen almost made me cry. Dirty dishes filled the
> sink and covered every inch of counter space. The high chair
> was smeared with gobs of banana. The floor was covered with
> the pots and pans I'd given to Darcy to play with so that I
> could get lunch for Nick. Now I'd have to wash them too.

Stay-at-home parents don't get a break either on Monday mornings or at the end of the conventional workweek on Fridays. While the working parent can escape the chaos of home, we who stay there must continue to face the seemingly endless onslaught of chores and chaos. This situation is a formula for chronic stress, which, if allowed to continue, will eventually damage our bodies, clutter our minds, harm our quality of life, and ultimately diminish our ability to parent effectively.

The Physiology of Stress

Our bodies are designed to respond to physical threats by triggering a physiological "fight or flight" response. This response causes the adrenal gland to secrete adrenaline and our pituitary gland to increase its production of the adrenocorticotropic hormone which stimulates the release of the hormone, cortisol. When the fight or flight response is triggered, the entire body is affected: digestion slows, breathing becomes rapid and shallow, muscles tense, perspiration increases, heartbeat accelerates, and senses become more acute.

This fight or flight response is advantageous if you are being chased by a rabid dog; but it is impracticable and inefficient for managing the daily chaos of parenting. Chronic levels of stress can lead to elevated blood pressure, irritable bowel syndrome, ulcers, nutritional deficiencies, teeth grinding, appetite changes, substance abuse, fatigue, diminished sexual drive, memory loss, heart disease, stroke, neck and back pain, sleep disturbances, headaches, and lowered immunity to disease. Stress can also manifest itself in psychological problems, including irritability, faulty problem solving, anxiety, and depression. According to Phyllis and James Balch's 1997 book, *Prescription for Nutritional Healing*, "Researchers estimate that stress contributes to as many as 80 percent of all major illnesses, including cardiovascular disease, cancer, endocrine and metabolic disease, skin disorders, and infectious ailments of all kinds."

Gasp! Aging

For those of us concerned about our appearance, new research suggests that stress may lead to premature aging. Dr. Elissa Epel and Dr. Elizabeth Blackburn of the University of California compared the DNA in white blood cells of women who were caretakers of disabled children to a control group of mothers of healthy children. *The New York Times* reported, "The researchers found that blood cells from women who had spent many years caring for a disabled child were, genetically, about a decade older than those from peers who had much less caretaking experience." Each time a cell reproduces itself to fight disease or repair its host organ, the cell's cap, called a telomere, shortens. At some point, the telomere becomes too short to reproduce, and the cell is retired. The longer a woman has been a caregiver, the shorter the length of her telomeres. Researchers also found that "the women who *perceived* [emphasis added] that they were under stress also had significantly shortened telomeres, compared with those who felt more relaxed—whether they were raising a disabled child or not."

Horrors! Body Fat

An increase in some hormones, including those produced in abundance when under stress, is now known to cause the body to store excess fat. According to neuroscientist Dr. Mary Dallman, "Increases in the absolute levels of both hormones (cortisol and insulin) result in the remodeling of body energy stores—away from muscle stores and toward fat stores, particularly abdominal fat stores."

Extreme Stress—My Story

Stress can negatively affect our parenting ability as well. In the summer of 2004, the southeastern coast of the United States was plagued by an alphabet soup of hurricanes. Week after week, one hurricane after another formed over the Atlantic Ocean and promptly headed—at least initially it seemed—straight for Savannah. Because our home is just a few miles inland and only a few feet above sea level, the risk was quite real. Frankly, I didn't handle it well. As each successive hurricane was projected to hit us, I found myself becoming increasingly irritable and edgy. I was not a pleasant person to be around. This ongoing stress built to a roaring crescendo when Hurricane Frances came knocking at the door, the fourth such storm in three weeks.

I lost it the morning my in-laws were scheduled to visit and the day before Hurricane Frances was projected to slam the Florida mainland south of us. I ran around the house preparing the children for school—at the same time helping the boys study for their spelling tests—at the same time fluffing pillows and scrubbing toilets for my soon-to-arrive guests—at the same time packing away precious photos for a possible evacuation. My baby was crying, so I put him in the playpen, where he quietly busied himself with his toys. We were running late, so I ordered the kids into the car, and we raced off to school.

We were halfway there when I turned around to check on my baby. He wasn't in his car seat! In a state of absolute panic, I turned the car around and flew home. I had ample time to imagine several worst-case scenarios: my house on fire, a social worker from the child protective agency at my front door, my baby dead in the playpen from some freak choking accident. I saw all of these images as I waited through red light after red light, berating myself the entire way. When I finally arrived home, I rushed in to find my baby sleeping peacefully in the playpen.

There is no escaping the stress of parenting. When children are babies, it's the stress of sleepless nights, the frequent near-death experiences, the emotional outbursts, and the random discharges of bodily fluid. As they grow older, it becomes the stress of fighting, whining, and the mass destruction of every possession you own and cherish. Of course, all of this is merely a warm-up for the teenage years, when we again return to the sleepless nights, the frequent near-death experiences, and the emotional outbursts. Finally, when the children do eventually move on and out, we often have to suffer the agony of watching them repeat all of our mistakes.

Picasso Stress

Comparing normal stress to parenting stress is like comparing the work of Rembrandt to that of Picasso. Parenting stress is normal stress with a queer cubistic twist. Here's an example: The day began with a routine visit to the grocery store. I placed my two oldest boys in the shopping cart and my young daughter in a baby backpack behind me. So far, everything was as it should be. My youngest son was sitting on a loaf of bread, while my other son repeatedly hit him over the head with a bag of cilantro. My daughter was busy plucking individual strands of hair from my head. Plink. Plink. Plink.

Despite these distractions, I remained focused on my quest. Down the aisles I raced, tossing item after item into the cart, oblivious to brand or price. I pulled two Gs around the corner as I spun my cart into the next aisle. I knew that at any moment, I might have to abort the operation, and I raced to beat the clock. Unfortunately, I lost.

It was in the soup section that I felt a warm, moist sensation running down my backside. I stopped to examine its source. To my horror, I observed the trail of diarrhea. It began at Maria's blown diaper, continued down my back, onto my leg, and, finally, to the floor. For a moment, I simply froze, my mind paralyzed by its inability to comprehend the truly unimaginable.

All I needed was a can of soup. With that, I would have completed my mission to the grocery store. I looked up from my cart to see an unsuspecting elderly gentleman shuffling in my direction. Quick! What's the protocol for such situations? Do I politely warn him of the mess? "Excuse me sir, you might want to detour!"

No, I didn't have the courage. Instead I pulled my boys out of the shopping cart and ran.

The Parent's Real-Life Stress Test

Rate the following ten conditions from 0 to 3. Zero is the equivalent of no stress, 3 denotes extreme stress. If the situation doesn't seem to apply, then it hasn't happened to you yet, but it will. Just rate those items a 3. Examples are provided.

_____ *Lack of sleep.* You haven't experienced even one night of uninterrupted sleep in the last six months, and your neighbors have just acquired a rooster that crows every morning at 4 am.

_____ *Spit-up.* Just as you are about to walk out the door, your baby sprays milk vomit from one sleeve of your recently dry-cleaned shirt to the other. You have nothing else to wear, of course, because you haven't had time to clean your other tops, also covered in spit-up.

_____ *Crying baby.* While waiting on hold for an hour to speak to someone about that mysterious charge on your phone bill, a real live person finally answers. At that moment, your baby suddenly takes a very deep breath and lets out a rip-roaring scream. The person on the other end pretends to not hear you and hangs up.

_____ *Whining children.* There is no relief. I'm a professional therapist and I've tried everything. Just give it a 3.

_____ ***Grocery shopping with children.*** Better that you all just starve than attempt this feat. (If you have actually tried to shop with children, you know as well as I do that this rates a 3.)

_____ ***Diaper blowouts.*** Just as you are about to load your baby into the car, he experiences a blowout. It's everywhere, from his little toes to his ears. As you wrestle to remove the defeated diaper, he suddenly kicks it out of your hand. In slow motion, the diaper flies into the air then flips itself poop-side down and lands on your favorite pumps. At this exact moment, you remember that you're out of diapers. (If you don't rate this a 3, you're from another planet.)

_____ ***Messes.*** You spend two hours cleaning your kitchen, taking advantage of that short holiday, called "naptime." You're just about to submerge yourself into a relaxing bubble bath, but first you pause to reflect on the magnificence of your work. Just at that moment, your oldest child and several of his friends come running through the door, leaving multiple tracks of mud that are traceable to the construction site down the street. Your bloodcurdling scream wakes the baby.

_____ ***Humility.*** In the rush to get your children to school, you failed to notice that your son had his shirt on inside out and backward and that a piece of neon green bubble gum was stuck in his hair.

_____ ***Unsolicited advice.*** At a family picnic, you attempt to surreptitiously breastfeed your baby. A distant relative spots you, and she walks all the way from the other side of the park to comment, "In my day, a woman kept her breast in her blouse where it belongs!" Three months later, at the family Christmas party, you are giving the same baby a bottle when a different relative approaches and says, "Oh dear, have you stopped breastfeeding already? That baby won't survive the winter!"

_____ **Lack of accomplishment.** You made a list of 15 things to accomplish today. You complete two of them but add 12 more. Your spouse returns home from work and sees only mayhem. He asks, "So what'd you do all day?"

Now tally up your score and check it against the benchmarks.

31 or higher You've been home too long, and it's time to take a refresher course in math.

21–30 You are completely stressed out, but at least you're honest. This chapter is mandatory reading. Have your blood pressure checked while you're at it.

11–20 Your stress level is moderate. You are alive and well-adjusted, but you should still read this chapter because I went through a lot of trouble to write it for you.

0 –10 Sorry. You weren't truthful in your responses. Please try again.

Stress-Busting Tools

Now that we've confirmed that you indeed need some form of relief, I'll present a few tools that will help you manage the stress.

Laugh

Perhaps you're wondering why I, a therapist and a person who professes to understand your pain, would poke fun at parental stress. After all, there is nothing humorous about diaper blowouts or intrusive relatives.

But the truth is, you may need to lighten up. Laughter is the most effective method of defusing a stressful situation. Laughing can lower our blood pressure, relax tense muscles, improve our breathing, and boost our immune system. Laughter also stimulates hormones that cause the brain to release endorphins, a natural opiate. When you allow yourself to laugh at a stressful situation, you defuse its power over you. Your body cannot interpret a situation as both dangerous and funny at the same time. Basically, when we take control over our interpretation of a situation, we tell our body how it should respond.

Control Environmental Sources of Stress

A home full of children is an obvious assault on our senses. Children yell, they scream, and they ruin the furniture. Environmental stimuli can compound this stress. Below are some examples:

Auditory   Chatter from the radio or television can intensify the noise level in the home. Seek to eliminate or reduce background noise whenever possible. Better yet, replace it with calming music.

Olfactory   Foul smells and odors exacerbate stress. Remove smelly diapers and other sources of offensive odors immediately. Open windows. Most of corporate America would kill for an office with a window, and here you have a dozen at home. Open them!

Visual   Clutter attacks our senses visually. Place a large attractive basket in each room for toys to make clean-up quick and easy for both you and your children. Accept the fact that messes are a natural by-product of having children. Remember, all over the world are parents just like you with small children, and they are dealing with the same problem. When you let go of your need for perfectionism, you also release the negative energy used to fight what is usually a losing battle. Try to celebrate the fact that messes are a reflection that your children are alive and thriving. Stop worrying about what other people think! Alternatively, you can create a visual sanctuary within your home, one or two rooms that are free of clutter, where your spouse can join you to find calm.

Tactile   Extremes in air temperature, both hot and cold, can also hamper our ability to handle stress. Poor-fitting shoes or tight clothing can also be aggravators, which is why comfortable jeans and sneakers are the "business casual" of the domestic diva circuit.

Reduce Internal Stressors

Stress levels can also be aggravated by our bodies' internal condition. Assess yourself. Are you hungry, thirsty, or tired? I've repeatedly found myself overresponding to stress at the same time that my body is screaming for a glass of water. With the chaos of four children, I know when I'm stressed, but I miss the simple fact that I'm thirsty.

Women are condemned to experience a regularly occurring event that should also be recognized. (Men, the following is for females only; please skip ahead to the next section.)

Ladies, we need to talk about psycho-day. Yeah, you know psycho-day. It's that interesting day that corresponds to the monthly arrival of our little friend. Oh, sure, you can deny the existence of such a day, but your husband knows the truth. In fact, he's an authority on the subject. It's possible that you may not recognize his expertise in this area because he never discusses the matter with you—for fear of his life.

Here's how it works for me. Several days before the onset of every menstrual period, I experience psycho-day. The problem is, I'm rarely aware that it's psycho-day until my husband cautiously points it out to me.

I'll call him at work, and the dialogue will go something like this:

I got a wrong number today. Can you believe it? Am I not busy enough that I have to answer the phone when it's the wrong number? Here I am trying to feed the baby. Then the phone rings. No, I mean it shrills, and I'm thinking, hey, it might be you. So I put the baby down and get up and answer it. And there's this lady on the end, right? She's trying to be sweet, asking if Mary Sue is there. And I say, "Hey! You have the wrong number!"

"Wow, that's horrible."
[Translation: Oh, great, here we go again.]

"Yeah, I know."

"Babe?" My husband will say in a hushed tone so the other guys in his office can't hear.

"Yeah, what is it?"

"I'm really sorry you had to experience that, but do you think it might be that day?" [Translation: I wonder how many more years before menopause begins.]

"What, Thursday?"

"No, you know, THAT day."

"Look, after the wrong number, I'm in no mood for this game. What are you trying to say?"

"Uh, you know, a psycho-day."

"Huh?" Pause. "Oh, yeah, I guess."

Unlike many of you, I'm not in denial about psycho-day. In fact, I am always relieved when I realize that it is, indeed, psycho-day. It means I won't have to be put in a straitjacket and carried away. It means whatever insanity has befallen me today will be gone tomorrow. Psycho-day is a good day to find a babysitter and just go shopping. There's no point in practicing stress management techniques or pretending to be rational. It's simply best to just grab your husband's checkbook, drop the baby at a sitter, and head to the mall for some "retail therapy."

Whether it's psycho-day or simply a bad hair day, we all have them, and, unfortunately, we can't always shop them away. On these days, we need to learn to slow our lives down. The world is not going to end if you miss a play date, have to reschedule an appointment, or don't pick up the phone every time it rings. Let someone else be the superhero.

Manage the Crying Baby

The cry of a baby can be an enormous stressor, especially for a new parent. The first point to remember is that all babies cry. In fact, some crying is considered healthy.

The needs and complaints of a baby are quite simple and fall into five general categories: sleep, diaper status, hunger/thirst, boredom, and pain or discomfort. When a child is crying, begin by ruling out each of these categories. While this procedure seems simplistic, it's easy to miss the obvious.

I recommend keeping babies on a flexible schedule, which means that the baby eats and sleeps at about the same times each day. Such a routine helps you to determine with increased confidence if hunger and tiredness are the underlying causes of your baby's cries. Numerous books can help you schedule your child, but don't become overly dogmatic or rigid about a routine or it will become a stressor in its own right. Used properly, flexible scheduling will bring some welcome order and predictability to you and your baby's lives.

If your baby's cries are overwhelming you, and you've ruled out the big five, put the baby down in a safe place, such as a crib, for a moment and attempt to calm down. Your baby is not going to suffer psychological trauma. Eventually, he or she will probably just fall asleep.

If your child cries more than three hours each day, he or she may have colic. Colic affects about 25 percent of all babies and begins as early as three weeks following birth. Colic can continue for several months.

The uncontrollable cry of a colicky baby can be very stressful, making us feel helpless, frazzled, and even a little crazy. Get help. Begin by talking to your child's pediatrician to rule out any health issues. Study coping techniques that work for both your baby and you and use them! Seek out friends or online support groups to give yourself a place to vent and to get much needed emotional support until this phase passes. Remember, you are not alone: over one million babies in the United States suffer from colic each year.

Learn to Say No

Learning to say no takes practice. This skill is particularly needed by stay-at-home parents because of a problem that seems to be unique to them: They're often viewed as a source of free labor by others.

Amy shares her experience:

I continue to be amazed at the way some working parents think nothing of treating me like a free babysitting or taxi service. It's sad, but I've had to terminate several relationships because I was clearly being used. The situation has happened so often, in fact, that I find myself almost paranoid when a working mother wants to befriend me. I immediately question her motives.

I encountered a similar problem many years ago after the birth of my first child, when a lady from church called to ask if I would contact each church family about an upcoming event—a project that would have required approximately 75 phone calls. I responded by saying that I would be happy to contact half of them. I actually heard her gasp before she asked in an incredulous tone, "Why, are you busy?" Truth was, yes I was busy—raising my baby—and I really wasn't in any mood to spend the rest of the month on the phone.

I had never before needed to defend how I chose to spend my time, but that clearly changed when I left my career to stay home.

Mary shares her story:

Every Wednesday, it's the same thing. I get a last minute call from my neighbor, who is always on business somewhere and needs me to take her daughter to dance. The other day she called just as I was leaving, so I didn't bother to answer the phone. Needless to say, her daughter never showed up for practice. When I told my husband the story, he said that it was a shame the poor little girl didn't make it to dance because of me. I said, "Excuse me? The girl didn't make it to dance because her parents didn't take her! I'd like to know when it became my job to chauffeur everyone else's kids around!"

Of course, sharing the load with other parents can be mutually beneficial, but be wary of those who may take purposeful advantage of your stay-at-home status. Search for partnerships that are equitable to both parties. While a fair and balanced arrangement can reduce the stress on everyone, a situation where you carry the bulk of the load will increase your stress and ultimately generate resentment.

Exercise

Exercise is one of the greatest perks readily available to the stay-at-home parent. Exercise not only reduces stress but it also increases your energy level, keeps you healthy, and ensures that you look fabulous. Exercise, like laughter, also releases endorphins and improves our ability to concentrate and sleep. Today, we have home gyms, exercise videos, jogging strollers, baby bike seats, and gym memberships that include child care. Stop making excuses!

Have Terrific Sex

Although sex is a great anxiety buster, sex can be the last thing on your mind after spending all day with children. Jenny, a mother of five, complains, "All day long, my kids are tugging, pulling, and climbing all over me. When my husband comes home from work and touches me, it makes me want to scream!"

The paradox is that, while stress may inhibit the desire for sex, sex itself is a great stress reliever. Like exercise and laughter, sex also releases endorphins. Calorie counters should note that sex burns up to 300 calories per exciting encounter. (Try to make it 400!) Research also shows that sex can be of particular benefit to men. According to a 1997 article in the *British Medical Journal*, men who have regular orgasms reduce their risk of premature death by a whopping 50 percent. Sex can also serve as a miracle sleep aid—just ask any woman who's tried to have a conversation with her husband after sex. Most important, sex can defuse the tension within a marriage that is so often exacerbated by children.

Find Respite

All parents need a reprieve. A grandparent, a friend, a spouse, a sitter, or a reliable day care center that takes drop-ins can all offer a much needed respite from our children. Some churches offer programs like "Parent's Day

Out," which are specifically designed for this purpose. Some parents find that taking turns babysitting each other's children is an economical way to gain some self-time.

You can also create a sanctuary within your own home. After your children are asleep, run yourself a hot bubble bath, light a few aromatic candles, grab a book, and refocus. I have a rule that I never clean after 9 pm. Once my children are asleep, that time is mine. I don't care how messy the house is. I find it necessary to know when my workday ends and when time for myself begins. Don't feel guilty about taking time for yourself.

Outsource the Nasty Stuff

Comedian Phyllis Diller once said, "Cleaning your house while your kids are still growing is like shoveling the walk before it stops snowing." The continual frustration of trying to keep your home clean and tidy when you have small children can be extremely exasperating and stressful. Consider outsourcing some of your more offensive chores. Even during those times when money is tightest, I send my husband's shirts to the cleaners to be washed and ironed. Having someone else do the work makes me feel like The Queen. Even a little outside help can reduce the stress at home.

Make the List

By its nature, parenting involves many small, seemingly insignificant tasks. In the everyday, we are often left with the feeling that we have little to show for our 24 hours. Begin by making a list of the items you plan to accomplish each day, including even the smallest tasks. If you give yourself credit only for the big achievements, you'll assume incorrectly that you have accomplished little and feel defeated.

Consider the words of English statesman and writer Sir Thomas More: "The ordinary arts we practice every day at home are of more importance to the soul than their simplicity might suggest."

Practice Deep Breathing

The following scenario is repeated daily somewhere on America's highways. Just as the vehicle passes the last rest stop for miles, traffic suddenly slows to a crawl, and a very squirmy three-year-old yells, "I gotta pee!" This is the time for deep breathing.

Deep breathing is a quick and easy way to help your body relax. The method is straightforward. Stand or sit up straight and inhale through your nose for a count of five seconds. Hold this breath for two seconds, then exhale through your mouth. Repeat this exercise several times, and your body will relax.

Control Your Self-Talk

Most of the stressors in modern life begin as faulty interpretations of our environment. If we say to ourselves, "Oh, my gosh, my child is about to pee in my car and no amount of Febreze can save me!" our bodies will respond with fear and anxiety. If, on the other hand, we reframe the event and say, "Oh, my gosh, my child is about to pee in my car! That means we might be able to buy a new minivan soon!" Our body says, "Yippie, a new minivan!" and hope and happiness replace anxiety and fear.

Our perception, or how we interpret our environment, can be just as damaging as the environment itself. Our minds have the power to create stress and the power to take it away. The next time you face a stressful situation, listen to your self-talk. You may be surprised to find that your thoughts consist of stress-inducing, critical, martyr-like whining: "I can't take this anymore!" or "Why is this happening to me?" Replace negative talk with power affirmations such as, "I can handle this!" You can also meditate on such calm-inducing words as "peace," or think calming thoughts such as, "I feel relaxed." These techniques are simple and they work.

Pray

Prayer can also be a powerful relaxation technique. James Balch, M.D. and Mark Stengler, N.D., authors of *Prescription for Natural Cures*, identify prayer as "the most powerful mind-body relaxation technique." Their opinion is validated in research conducted by Duke University Medical Center. A study of 4,000 participants over the age of 65 found that those who prayed and attended weekly religious services had lower blood pressure than those who did not.

Maintain Perspective

Pause and examine the contributions you make to your own stress. Ask yourself whether today's pressures and concerns will matter by next week. A month from now? In five or 10 years? Without realizing it, we create a self-defeating frenzy of worry. Avoid the tendency to make problems bigger than they actually are.

Get Your Sleep

It has been said that people who sleep like a baby usually don't have one. According to the American Psychological Association, the average person needs about eight hours of sleep to ensure sound mental and physical health. Because sleep is vital to your mental health, you should avoid the urge to stay up very late to catch up on chores. In addition, you would do well to practice napping. The short time lost is more than traded for the enhanced energy and increased performance that results from the nap.

Tracy, former teacher and a mother of four, offers an interesting metaphor: "Flight attendants tell us that, in an emergency, we need to put on our oxygen masks before our children's. It's the same concept with napping. When we take care of ourselves, we're better able to take care of our children."

Eat Well

Chronic stress can also lead to nutritional deficiencies through overexcretion of vital nutrients, interfering with their absorption and disrupting the way we eat. Dr. Elissa Epel, an assistant professor at the University of California, San Francisco (UCSF), says, "Stress causes some people to eat more, some to eat less. Stress disrupts our homeostasis. The same neural networks that regulate appetite and satiety also regulate the stress response."

Stress can also lead to unhealthy food choices. Laurel Mellin, associate clinical professor of family and community medicine and pediatrics at UCSF, states, "When insulin levels and cortisol levels increase, the tendency is to eat sugar, fat, and salty, crunchy foods. Unfortunately the kinds of foods we crave when our cortisol and insulin levels are up only add to the weight gain."

Without intervention, a vicious cycle begins wherein stress depletes your nutritional reservoirs at the same time that it causes cravings for still more nutritionally empty foods. These deficiencies then further weaken your body's ability to cope with future stress, and the cycle is repeated.

Being at home has the downside of unrestricted access to the food in your kitchen. Hence, your refrigerator should contain healthy food choices, including whole grains, legumes, vegetables, and fresh fruits. Your children will also benefit from the availability of these healthy choices.

Practice Visualization

Visualization is the art of closing your eyes and picturing a place of comfort and peace. For some, it might be a tropical beach, for others, a view of a snowcapped mountain. This place can be real or imaginary. Sit down, close your eyes, and let your mind take you on a refreshing mini vacation.

Watch the Caffeine

Coffee and I have a special relationship. It's called addiction. I absolutely love coffee: the flavors, the aroma, the intellectual ambience at the java shops. I tried quitting coffee once and was stunned to discover that, for me, coffee is more than a hot beverage, it is an integral part of my personality.

Of course, coffee contains caffeine, which can help make a person tense and irritable and exacerbate stress. Consequently, stress reduction and sleep are going to be more challenging if you are simultaneously pumping yourself with a stimulant, so moderate your intake accordingly. I've recently had to stop drinking caffeinated beverages before mid-afternoon to assure that I get a good night's sleep.

Simplify Your Life

The energy we once applied to our careers does not magically disappear when we become stay-at-home parents. For this reason, new stay-at-home parents often attempt to fill every spare minute with some sort of project, mission, or activity. Their problem isn't saying no; it's saying please. Please give me something to do!

After dedicating years to their jobs, goal-oriented career people have difficulty slowing down. And while there's nothing wrong with redefining yourself and enjoying new tasks in your spare time, it's important not to lose the focus of why you are home: to benefit your children. If you create too much busyness, your children naturally become an inconvenience and a hindrance to your goals. The days when your children are little should be a time of simplicity.

Of course, none of these recommendations will be of any use if you are a bona fide stress seeker. In other words, if you're constantly complaining about the amount of stress you're under, the truth is that stress may actually be serving an important purpose in your life. If you are unwilling to let go of your stress, you may be a stress seeker.

People become stress seekers for several reasons. Similar to coffee, stress gives us a rush of energy that keeps us flying through our day with great enthusiasm. The addiction-like hold of stress may lie in its chemical release of energy hormones such as adrenaline. Without this rush, we may find ourselves feeling tired or bored.

A state of constant stress also makes us feel important and valuable. Sure, we're home, but we're busy! If we're not busy enough, then we'll have a few more kids, toss in a shoe-chewing puppy, and begin working on our second Ph.D. If we discover 15 minutes of daily free time, we'll start a home-based business or solve world hunger. Our resistance to simply relaxing may be an unconscious effort to mask feelings of depression or low self-worth—feelings that are common when parents step away from their careers.

Acknowledge your role in creating your own stress, and no longer play victim to it. Any reluctance to let go of stress should be analyzed. Ask yourself, "Why am I refusing to let go of my stress? What are the benefits of holding onto it? Are uncomfortable feelings lurking beneath the frenzy of my activity?"

Don't Add Pets to the Mix

Shortly after the birth of my second child, I stumbled across a woman who was giving away cute little puppies in front of a department store. I must have been deranged by hormones, because, at the time, I actually thought it would be a great idea to take one of them home. So I asked the woman to identify the puppy with the calmest disposition. She pointed to Shadow.

My first mistake was failing to ask Tim if he'd mind if I brought a dog home. Saying he wasn't happy would be an understatement. It didn't help that Shadow cried all night long—for days on end. The morning after bringing her home, as my sleep-deprived husband stumbled through the darkness to get ready for work, he stepped in not one but three piles of doggy diarrhea. You see, Shadow wasn't as mellow as her former owner implied. She was ill. Once she recovered, it went downhill from there.

Shadow quickly became the Houdini of dogs. She could break free of any form of entrapment within seconds. She could scale her six-foot high pen with ease, slip out of chokers, and withstand the shock of her electric collar. You name it; we tried it. And when she escaped, which was several times a day, she'd run through the mountains looking for things to chew: neighbors' shoes, water hoses, children's bicycles, newly planted trees. Nothing was safe from her oral fixation. If Tim and I happened to be driving down our rural road and saw a neighbor's trash spewed across their yard, we'd automatically stop and clean it up because we knew who did it. Shadow was out of control, and our neighbors weren't happy about it.

The work associated with my second baby was nothing compared to the work associated with Shadow. After two years of hoping she'd grow up, we sent her off to a relative with more pet patience than we were able to muster.

I share this story because I've seen it time and again. Like cake and ice cream, babies and puppies just naturally seem to go together. But I've repeatedly watched friends with the best of intentions ultimately give away recently adopted pets when it became clear that they couldn't manage two "babies" at the same time.

Because the first few years of your child's life can be particularly challenging, I recommend that you wait until your youngest is at least three years old before adding a new pet to the family. Trust me on this one.

Peace

Parenting can be stressful. Although we can't change all of the stressors associated with parenting, we can work to change our attitude and improve our coping skills.

An anonymous author leaves us with this thought:

Peace.
It does not mean to be in a place
where there is no noise,
trouble,
or hard work.
It means to be in the midst of those things
and still be calm in your heart.

CHAPTER 10

Facing Fickle Finances

*Most of the luxuries and many of the
so-called comforts of life are not only not
indispensable, but positive hindrances to
the elevation of mankind.*

~Henry David Thoreau

Let me begin this chapter by confessing that I am not a financial expert, nor could I ever become one. I have one of those brains that flits about from idea to idea, rebelling like a restless two–year–old when it's forced to sit still and work a budget spreadsheet.

So, while this chapter covers some economic basics and a few money-saving tips, its primary purpose is to introduce you to the philosophical mind-set of the single-income family. By adopting this mind-set, you will be able to create your own strategies that will help you manage the dramatic changes to your budget following your loss of income. They will help you resist the pull of a materialistic world.

Facing the Facts

No matter how you do the math, two incomes minus one income equals one income. This simple equation means that you should expect that your decision to leave your career will have immediate and long-lasting consequences. Your day-to-day standard of living, your vacation destinations, and even the brand of toilet paper you choose may all be affected by this decision.

Your ability to fund investments such as retirement, life insurance, and property could also be altered. So, while you may be home for what will only be a fraction of your lifetime, your decision is likely to have repercussions well into the future. I recently read an article by a financial expert encouraging stay-at-home moms to contribute 3,000 tax-free dollars each year to their retirement. Great advice, but how many one-income families can easily dig up that kind of extra money each year?

In addition to the loss of income, your expenses increase dramatically due to the cost of raising children. The Department of Agriculture, which conducts consumer expenditure surveys on the cost of child rearing, estimates that families can expect to spend between $134,000 and $270,000 to raise a child from birth through age 17. The per year expenditure for a child under age two is between $7,000 and $15,000.

But Can We Really Live on One Income?

You might be thinking this wasn't a very encouraging way to start a chapter about finances. After all, who really can afford moving to one income after becoming accustomed to two? But when I consider whether it is possible for most families to survive on one income, I think back to my friend, Suzie.

Suzie was a single mother of four children. Her first three children were older, from a previous marriage. And her fourth? He was a surprise. But Suzie decided she would give her fourth son the gift she had given her first three and stay home with him during his early years. As a single mother, she relied only on sporadic child support and an occasional odd job.

There is no question that Suzie's financial problems were constant. She was often late on her rent, and her utility bills frequently went unpaid. It wasn't uncommon for me to try to reach her by phone or e-mail only to discover that her services had been cut off. But Suzie made it work, and while I certainly would never encourage anyone to live on the edge the way Suzie did, her life brought renewed perspective to my own. Indeed, she practiced, even mastered, the art of living without. And above all else, Suzie managed to remain a stay-at-home mother to the benefit of her son.

My purpose in presenting Suzie's story is to show what is possible, even in an extreme case, when a mother makes the decision to be home with her child. Most families would not be faced with such a dire financial predicament should they lose a source of income, especially if they honestly assess the resources necessary for a reasonable standard of living.

When evaluating your ability to handle income loss, you should consider the frame of reference that might be biasing your thought process. For instance, if you find yourself constantly comparing your material worth against that of your neighbors or family members, you might find it very difficult to let go of your current income. If this is true, try to change your mental reference points.

As an example, the loss of one income would mean a significant reduction in housing options for many families. But would this really be a problem for yours? Robert Rector shed light on America's obsession with home living space in an article from the October 25, 1999, *National Review*: "On average, America's poor have 440 square feet of living space per person. This is more than the average citizen in Paris, Berlin, and London; nearly three times the average in the capitals of such nations as Poland and Mexico."

The same article also lucidly illustrates that even most people at the poverty level in America have a better standard of living than do citizens of average income in other developed countries. This suggests that it might be advantageous to continuously ask ourselves the question, what do we really need?

If it means being able to stay home with our children, do we need that larger home in a more expensive neighborhood? Can we give up yearly vacations to extravagant locales when a short trip to the beach, mountains, or desert could be just as fulfilling for the family? Could we sell one of our cars or buy used next time, instead of new? Can we make public education work for our children in lieu of expensive private schooling? Are we willing to eat out less often? Would our level of contentment really be any different if we cut back on our spending habits?

As we move on to look at our budget, I encourage you to honestly consider what your needs really are and what you'd be willing to sacrifice to be able to successfully make the move from career to home.

The Budget

Before making a change of this magnitude, it's essential that you sit down with your spouse and scrutinize your new budget-to-be. As you examine your current spending habits, don't forget those places where money may be trickling away unnoticed. For example, if you enjoy treating yourself to a $4 vanilla latte once a day, this seemingly innocent passion will cost you over $100 each month or more than $1,000 a year. Probably not an issue if you're working, but possibly a big deal if you're not.

If your new budget falls in the red, the question obviously becomes: what can be eliminated? If you have nothing left to cut and no practical way to further reduce your expenses, perhaps transitional income will be necessary until your financial situation stabilizes. (Part-time work is covered in chapter 11.)

If you find your new budget a little depressing, consider creating a "What If" version that reflects your expenses if you did continue to work. In this budget scenario, you include expenses associated with your career, such as child care, transportation, clothing, eating out, and higher income taxes. In comparison, your single-income budget may not look so bad after all.

What Is an Alma Worth?

Even though you may not be earning tangible income, your time at home is worth more than you think. Salary.com recently evaluated the duties associated with the stay-at-home mother and combined these to obtain a monetary value. They concluded:

> Stay-at-home mothers wear many hats. They're the family CEO, the day care provider, accountant, chauffeur, counselor, chef, nurse, laundress, entertainer, personal stylist, and educator. Based on a 100-hour work week, Salary.com has estimated that a fair wage for the typical stay-at-home mom would be $131,471 for executing all of her daily tasks.

While salary.com's formula may appear to be a bit patronizing, it does acknowledge the numerous duties associated with the job, the amount of time dedicated to these duties, and an appreciation of the value of the work we do.

Adopting the Single-Income Mind-Set

Moving from two incomes to one may require that you change the way you think about money. Our income is often used as a gauge with which we define our status in the workplace or our position in society. Our income gave us an element of power. It paid for nice dinners, vacations, and clothing. To leave that all behind can be difficult. Indeed, to do so requires that we embrace the following five virtues:

Virtue 1: Sacrifice—Staying at home to raise your children requires sacrifice. It is this same sacrifice that causes stay-at-home parents to recoil when they are told that they are "fortunate," "blessed," or "lucky" to be home. While they may be blessed, indeed, most families make major sacrifices to be so.

I still recall the moment I came to fully realize the sacrifice I was making to be home. Shortly after the birth of my second son, Michael, my husband and I drove from our mountain home in Tehachapi, California, to the lowlands of Bakersfield to pick up hardware supplies. The air conditioner in our car was broken, and we couldn't afford to have it repaired. This wasn't an issue in the cooler climate of the mountains, but it became a definite problem on this scorching August day down in Bakersfield.

When we arrived at the hardware store, I needed to feed the baby. Tim parked in the shade of a eucalyptus tree and left with our oldest child, James, to purchase supplies. The tree provided little relief from the unbearable summer heat. While I breastfed Michael, sweat dripped into my eyes, mouth, and onto the baby. Michael, who was also sweating profusely, was literally stuck, skin-to-skin, to my belly.

I happened to look over at the car beside me and, in what can only be described as an odd coincidence, noticed that the woman inside was also breastfeeding her baby. For a brief few seconds I couldn't help but stare at the contented mother. I watched her smile peacefully as she looked down at her baby, a light wisp of dry hair dancing lightly about her face from the cool breeze of her *working* air conditioner. I thought to myself, "What has happened to my life that I ended up in this car?"

For most stay-at-home moms, financial survival is synonymous with sacrifice. Depending on the income of your working spouse, where you live, and how many children you have, the amount of sacrifice will vary.

Jenny is a teacher and a mother of five. Her family manages to live on the single income of her husband, who is also a teacher. For her, survival has been all about sacrifice:

> We don't have "stuff." We don't have decent furniture, nice clothes, or nice cars. Sure, those things would be great, but they aren't a priority over our family. We usually manage to take some sort of vacation, but not always. We never get to go to neighborhood festivals in the summer because we can't afford the rides. We have a large list of home improvements that we want to do, but have to say, "Well, someday ..."

> We buy generic brand food. Always. We shop at K-Mart and Wal-Mart instead of Kohl's and Dillard's. We gladly accept hand-me-down clothes. I shop for toys at yard sales.

> We don't think our kids are lacking. They are active in sports, do great in school, and we are involved in their lives. They know they are number one with us. They will only be little for such a short time! What I'm doing by being home is much more important to us than "stuff."

Michelle is the wife of a veterinarian, mother of three, and a veterinarian herself. But even she has had to make sacrifices:

> We don't eat out. I cook often from scratch. We never take fancy vacations. I buy furniture from Goodwill and I spruce it up with paint. I never pay full price for any big item. Many stores will bargain with you, and I'm not afraid to ask.

> We never carry a balance on our credit cards. If we can't afford to pay them off every month, then we don't make the

*purchase. Window shopping is dangerous because I always
end up spending more than I should have, so I stay out of
stores unless I have a list. We buy used cars and pay for them
in cash if possible.*

*Finally, we tithe at church. I don't know how we are able to
make ends meet in doing so, but we do.*

Virtue 2: Humility—I was in line at Goodwill once when the phone belonging to the lady in front of me began to ring. She picked it up and said, "Oh, hi! Well, I'll be there in about fifteen minutes. I'm at the mall." I thought of yelling, "Don't believe her! She's in line with us undesirables at Goodwill!" I find no shame in shopping at Goodwill. In fact, had I taken the call, it probably would have sounded like this: "Girlfriend, guess where I am? I'm at Goodwill, and you would not believe the deals today!"

Be proud of your humble lifestyle!

Virtue 3: Simplicity—A life of simplicity is in many ways a spiritual quest, one that requires that we separate ourselves from a world obsessed with having the newest, biggest, and best. The goal of simplicity is to find peace in a walk that is often far different from that of the others around you. While your working friends and neighbors may be buying bigger homes, dressing their children in brand-name clothes, and enjoying fabulous vacations, you on the other hand may be downsizing your home, dressing your children in hand-me-downs, and selling family heirlooms to pay the phone bill. To find peace in this means that we are not envious, angry, or bitter about the absence of things we've chosen to live without.

Virtue 4: Humor—I believe that one of the reasons my friend Suzie survived her low-income years at home was that, no matter how bad things became, she always maintained a sense of humor.

I have to admit that it took us a while before we could see the humor in the used minivan we purchased a few years back. Following the birth of our third baby, Maria, we immediately needed a vehicle with more seating than our old SUV provided. We promptly went out and bought ourselves a heavily used lemon.

Within a short time, everything that could possibly break on that death trap did. From the air conditioner to the transmission, from the power windows to the suspension, one-by-one, front to back, side to side, things just fell apart. Like a doctor working triage, Tim desperately tried to keep up with the repairs, only to have something else break immediately.

Our ongoing problems with the van went from distressing to absurd when the passenger door spontaneously rusted itself from the hinge followed by the total failure of all the dashboard instruments. We improvised to get by. The passenger door was held shut by duct tape and a rope tied to the inside handle. Vehicle speed was estimated by the sound of the wind blowing over the van. Finally, the transmission failed, putting an end to the year-long battle. The clunker was towed off by a charity; we couldn't believe the organization wanted it. The fellow at work who sold Tim the vehicle could never look him in the eye again.

We certainly don't always appreciate the humor at the time, but our low-income adventures eventually provide ample material for chuckles down the road.

Virtue 5: Gratitude—When we are always in a state of want, we fail to appreciate what it is we already have. Instead of comparing yourself to those who have more, think of those who have less and be grateful for the blessings you do have.

Thou Shalt Not Covet Thy Neighbor's GMC V8 Suburban with Leather Interior, Tinted Sunroof, and Built-In Baby Seats—

One of the more difficult challenges to our resolve comes from envy. As we watch our neighbors and friends enjoying the finer things in life, it is easy to assume that they must be happier than we are. But much of the research on the subject conflicts with this premise. Dr. Ed Diener has spent much of his career studying the phenomenon of subjective well-being (SWB) and wealth. In "Will Money Increase Subjective Well-Being?" he and Robert Biswas-Diener conclude: "It appears that a higher income might help if we are very poor. Gaining more income if we are middle-class or upper-class and are living in a wealthy nation is unlikely to substantially bolster our SWB on a long-term basis."

What this means for most of us is that, while our friends and neighbors may, indeed, drive nicer cars, wear better clothing, and live in larger homes, it is unlikely that they are actually happier than we are, assuming again that our essential needs are being met.

Now, what if your basic needs are being met, yet you find yourself experiencing a great deal of monetary discontent? What, then, is the source? Dr. Tim Kasser's research may have your answer: "When people believe materialistic values are important, they report less happiness and more distress, have poorer interpersonal relationships, contribute less to the community, and engage in more ecologically damaging behaviors."

You may, indeed, be less happy, but it is not the lack of money that is ultimately to blame. It is more likely to be your own emphasis on materialism. If this is you, step back. Train your focus away from stuff and, instead, concentrate your attention on life's more important commodities.

Tips for Financial Survival

Making ends meet on one income is a daily art, one that requires creativity and humility. The following are some suggestions you may want to try to cut your costs.

Use Coupons—I've saved an enormous amount of money using coupons over the years. I was in line at the grocery store recently and happened to have an unusually large number of them. The gentleman in line behind me was very patient while he watched in silent awe as the grocer swiped coupon after coupon after coupon. When the tired grocer was finally finished, she said in a rather annoyed voice, "You saved fifty-one dollars and forty cents." She may not have appreciated it, but a resounding "Wow!" came from the man behind me. And let me tell you, this is big money in my home.

Some people despise using coupons or choose to patronize stores that supposedly price their merchandise so low as to not accept them. But if you are serious about using coupons, you can find them just about anywhere: in magazines, the Sunday paper, local business advertising booklets, and online. You can also contact companies directly and request coupons. This is particularly valuable for expectant mothers. Once you learn that you are pregnant, contact every baby business you can think of and inform them that you're expecting. Toy, food, clothing, and formula companies will not only send you generous coupons but free products as well. Even if you're not planning on using formula, get connected with formula companies, because you may change your mind in the future or need a backup when a babysitter fills in.

Don't Fear Generic Foods—Sometimes I'm just too busy to deal with coupons, so I focus my attention instead on generic brands when I'm at the store. Not all generic brands are of the same caliber as name brands. Some are downright terrible. But I've learned which stores' generic items are of high quality. And most generic diapers are more than adequate: as long as they seal properly, your child is only going to poop in them!

Along these same lines, I often find myself shopping at stores I don't otherwise care for simply because the prices are better. With six in the household, I buy a lot of groceries, and even modest differences in pricing on individual items can add up quickly. With these savings, I can justify the purchase of higher-grade foods like organic milk and fruit, items that our kids consume a lot of.

Make Your Own Baby Food—Baby food is easy to make. Instead of spending 60 cents a jar on name brand, I made most of my children's baby food from scratch. Sweet potatoes, for example, can be cooked, blended, stored in old baby jars, and frozen for later use. Even dinners like spaghetti or soup can be blended and stored in this manner. Making your own baby food not only lowers your food bill, but it can also expose your child to a greater variety of fresh foods with higher nutritional content and fewer additives.

If you don't want the hassle of making your own food, just remember that your baby's food does not have to always come in expensive little glass jars. For example, you can save money by purchasing a large container of organic sugar-free applesauce instead of the smaller jars that contain barely one serving. Special juices and treats marketed for babies are generally overpriced and are not necessarily any healthier.

If you do choose to venture outside of the baby aisle, be sure to follow your pediatrician's advice for transitioning your child to solid foods.

Avoid Shopping with Children—If possible, avoid shopping with your children. Babies add a sense of urgency, making it difficult to compare prices and use coupons. Older kids can whine you into buying junk that you don't need or want. In the chaos of shopping with kids, I've even come home with items I didn't realize I had purchased and missed purchasing items I really needed.

Buy Secondhand—If you are an admitted clothes snob, this might be a good time to break yourself of the habit. Many stay-at-home moms rely heavily on secondhand clothing. Children grow fast, they're quick to ruin their clothes, and the seasons are always changing. Secondhand clothing can be found at consignment shops and yard sales, on eBay, or from friends. I make it a point to ask acquaintances if I can purchase their children's used clothing items once they're through with them. Sometimes, they'll sell them to me at a great price; and other times, they simply pass along the clothes in the same manner that I often give mine away.

Tim and I also buy all of our vehicles preowned. I recall an ad recently that reminded listeners, "everyone drives a used car." How true. Not only are new cars a notoriously bad investment, children have a way of devaluing them in such a manner that owning one can feel like experiencing water drip torture. I personally like having the "first dent" already in place. That way, when one of the kids rides his bike straight into the side of the car, it doesn't bother me as much.

Garage Sale Hop—The best deals on baby items are almost always found at garage sales. When I was pregnant with my first child, I hit a single garage sale where I purchased nearly everything I needed to prepare for the birth of my son. These items included a crib, changing table, toys, even an old video camera, and all for less than $150.

At another sale, I bought a beautiful rustic swing set made from lodgepole pine for only $10. The seller even delivered and installed it for free! That inexpensive swing set survived deep snowdrifts in the California mountains, termites and subzero weather in Ohio, and the move to Georgia, only to be washed into a canal and out to the Atlantic Ocean during a terrific rainstorm soon after our arrival in Savannah. A tragic story, but it shows what you can get for ten bucks!

Back in my days as a pro, I had a system for attacking the garage circuit. During the week, I'd pick up a local paper and scan the garage sale section. I'd determine the location of each and its start time. With map in hand, I'd plan to hit each one just before "official" opening, knowing that the best stuff is usually gone within the first hour. ("Early birds" may be annoying, but, hey, they get the goods.)

Because garage sale hopping can be hit or miss, it's important to make it fun. Over the years, I've turned it into a social event. Sometimes I'll meet a friend before sunrise, and, with coffee in hand, we'll head out. It's also a great way to meet new people. I recently participated in a neighborhood garage sale and was pleasantly surprised to have an actor from a major play we had recently attended show up in our driveway.

Buy Off-Season and When the Deals Are Hot—Buying at the moment of need is a very inefficient way to shop. You can expect to pay far more for a coat in the fall than you would if you bought it in spring. Realizing this, when I find a great deal on something, I buy it then and there if I'm sure that I'll need it in the future. It's not uncommon for me to purchase children's clothing far in advance of when it will be worn. While this may seem a little silly at first thought, kids grow up fast, and it's a pleasant relief to open a box years later to find all kinds of wonderful clothes ready for your child to wear.

Learn to Cut Hair—Master of the Bowl Cut used to be my title until a neighbor was kind enough to teach me how to trim hair properly. It's much simpler than you might think, and you can save a significant amount of money over time. At an average cost of over $10 per head, I figure I save hundreds of dollars each year. All it takes is a hair-cutting kit from the department store, and you're on your way.

While I do trim my children's hair, I can't seem to convince Tim to let me cut his. The problem stems from a deeply ingrained memory he has of a former coworker who came to work one day with large sections of his hair missing. Apparently, his spouse had become distracted and placed the razor setting a little too low. Being the nice guy that he was, he chose not to hurt his wife's feelings and opted for "business as usual." His coworkers, on the other hand, did their part by avoiding eye contact. But foul-ups of this magnitude are the exception, not the rule.

To be fair to Tim, I also no longer attempt to do my own hair. After years of searching for inexpensive ways to do so from home, including my personal favorite—total neglect—I've come to the conclusion that hiring a professional is worth it. I have used beauty schools, which generally offer salon services for a fraction of the price, but there is an element of risk when you entrust your hair to a student. Remember: hair is not like armpit fat; you can't hide it.

But we're talking about children's hair here, not yours or your husband's. So learn how to perform kiddy cuts and save.

Grow a Garden—A yard full of vegetables, herbs, and fruit trees is a fun way to take the edge off the grocery bill while teaching your child to appreciate the miracle of food. My son, who has despised store-bought tomatoes since the day he was born, will eat handfuls of them from his dad's garden.

Enjoy Being Home—There is no doubt that you can save a great deal of money by eating out less often. Although we definitely believe in going out on dates occasionally, it can be quite expensive, easily exceeding $100 when we factor in a nice meal, maybe a movie, and child care. We find it just as fun and far cheaper to buy a bottle of wine, rent a good movie, and just hang out after the kids are asleep.

When we do go out on the town, especially with all of the kids in tow, we seek less expensive alternatives. Some restaurants offer a "kids' night" in which the children's meals are free. I keep a purse full of restaurant coupons, which helps us focus on where we might eat that evening. Instead of always ordering one of the stereotypically unhealthy options on the kid's menu, we frequently request a separate plate and share healthier entrees with our kids. On those rare occasions when we all go see a movie at the theater, we attend a discounted matinee. At work, Tim generally avoids leaving for lunch and, instead, eats leftovers from our previous meals that I have frozen in microwavable containers.

Know the Tax Benefits—You can save tremendously on your income taxes when you understand your benefits as a family. To make sure you haven't missed a critical deduction, purchase good computer tax return preparation software or hire a certified public accountant. If you are unfamiliar with the tax code, investing in a CPA is money in the bank. Your CPA is likely to save you a surprisingly large amount on your taxes while instructing you on the basics that you can then use to complete your own returns in the future.

Cut Back on Driving—Our older children are engaged in numerous after-school activities, so I do a lot of driving. Because gas is becoming increasingly expensive, I group school activities and errands into single trips whenever possible.

Avoid Temptation—Since I spend a great deal of time at the computer, online stores and auctions remain a constant temptation. While I can often score incredible deals, the ease of shopping online makes it easy to overspend, especially on unnecessary items. So I always have to keep my guard up, especially when I'm bored.

To avoid the temptation of catalogs that come in the mail, toss them into the recycling bin before reading them or put your name on a national no-junk-mail list. I've even set limits on how much I contribute to school fund-raisers, although what I don't provide to schools in money, I do attempt to make up for in service.

Ask for Help When You Need It—While I certainly don't advocate that you turn your time at home into an excuse to leach from family, neighbors, or church, I do think there are occasions when it's absolutely proper to ask for help.

I jokingly refer to our financial state as "large family poverty." While we really are not impoverished, we are also not wealthy in that we have limited discretionary money available at the end of the month. So, while it would be nice to send my kids to a week of summer camp, for example, we simply can't afford it with four children. However, many businesses and organizations that serve children understand that parenting can be very expensive and offer scholarships, discounts, or sliding-fee scales to those families that need or ask for them. Don't be afraid to ask whether discounts or grants are available.

If you'd feel uncomfortable about accepting aid from such organizations, it may help if you'd commit to patronize them at a later date should you return to work or once your financial situation improves.

Pray—Now when I say, "pray for your finances," I definitely do not mean that you should live irresponsibly, expecting God to clean up your messes. On the other hand, I am suggesting that, as you go about living sensibly, you should pray when you have a need.

Here is a recent example of how powerful prayer can be: When we were living in Cincinnati, I was part of an informal group of four mothers who were very supportive of one another. We passed along maternity clothes, baby items, breast pumps, and the like. If you needed it, someone was able to find it for you.

After we moved to Savannah from Cincinnati, however, I no longer had that support system. And while I continued to give away bags of my children's clothing, very little was coming back. When I discovered that I was into my last box of secondhand clothing from Cincinnati, I found myself panicking. How was I going to afford to buy new clothes for four children?

So I prayed about it. I confess that this particular prayer may have sounded a little too business-like. I said, "God, I'm giving away hundreds of dollars worth of clothing and getting little back. You know I cannot make ends meet without secondhand clothing, so if you could help me out here, I'd really appreciate it!"

By the end of the month, I had four women give me nearly a dozen boxes full of clothes, toys, and other miscellaneous items. The outpouring of support was so overwhelming that I couldn't help but laugh. It was as if God wanted to make it very clear to me that this largesse came from Him. I no longer had to be concerned about how I would purchase next year's wardrobe for my two-year-old. Instead I had the very desirable problem of trying to figure out how to store the clothes that will serve him until he's seven!

Barter—Instead of looking at how you can afford to pay for everything, consider ways to barter. Perhaps you could trade your professional skills for a service you can't afford right now. Or you might offer to watch someone's child in exchange for something you need, like clothing or furniture.

Don't Confuse Money with Love—Advertisers are on a mission to convince you and your children that happiness comes from material things. Remember the Tickle Me Elmo craze? Out of the blue, for no apparent reason other than herd mentality, Christmas in 1996 was not complete without the overpriced fuzz ball with a vibrating microchip. Demand was so high that parents were paying thousands of dollars to make sure their little bundles of joy had one of these apparently indispensable dolls. Were their children grateful? Heck no. They knew it was lame the moment they set eyes on it.

Money is a poor way to express your love. Instead teach your children that there are monetary limits in life. They'll learn to accept this reality and rarely be disappointed. On the contrary, it builds character. As Willy Wonka would be the first to tell you, children who get everything they want eventually become incorrigible brats.

You don't have to spend a lot of money to have a great time with your kids. Have a picnic in the park, ride your bike, or hike a trail. Sit down with some clay, paint a birdhouse, or string some beads together. Let go of the guilt of not being able to buy your children everything they want. It will be the time spent together, not the money spent at the store, that your children will remember.

Worth More than Gold

The transition from two incomes to one requires that we not only adjust our finances, but also our philosophy regarding money. To do this, we must reject the world's materialistic perspective and tightly grasp the greater purpose of life. This requires maturity, patience, and sacrifice, some of which only comes with the passage of time. In the meantime, we must hold firm to our values and weather the financial storms. The benefits of our time at home may be intangible, but its worth is far greater than gold.

I leave you with words of an anonymous prophet: "One hundred years from now, it will not matter what kind of house I lived in, how much money I had, nor what my clothes were like. But the world may be a little better because I was important in the life of a child."

CHAPTER 11

To Work or Not to Work

*Imagine life as a game in which you
are juggling five balls in the air. You
name them—work, family, health,
friends, and spirit—and you're keeping
all of these in the air. You will soon
understand that work is a rubber ball.
If you drop it, it will bounce back. But
the other four balls—family, health,
friends, and spirit—are made of glass.
If you drop one of these, they will be
irrevocably scuffed, marked, nicked,
damaged, or even shattered. They will
never be the same. You must understand
that and strive for balance in your life.*

*~Brian Dyson, CEO of Coca Cola
Enterprises, 1959–1994*

While it may seem contrary to include a chapter on work in a book for stay-at-home mothers, I don't believe it is. In fact, I think it's fair and proper to call oneself a stay-at-home mother and still work outside the home. My sense is that the ongoing hostility between stay-at-home mothers and career mothers could be greatly diminished if we acknowledge that there is, indeed, a third solution to the work-and-home dilemma, and this is part-time work. It is also my belief that if more part-time work options were available, it would reduce the number of women who feel compelled to rush back into a full-time career.

You are probably wondering what my concept of part-time work is. I suppose I'll just have to frustrate you by saying … it depends. "Part time" is certainly meant to imply something less than the standard, and typically family-unfriendly, 40-hour work week.

But part-time hours won't necessarily be any easier on you or your family if you don't enjoy the work or if your hours conflict with the schedules of your spouse and children. When I worked weekends, I usually didn't exceed 10 hours per week. Tim was home with the kids then, but as few as these hours were, they seemed to stymie month after month of fun together as a family, along with any hope of relaxation. Some mothers, on the other hand, may have options that permit them to squeeze far more hours into their week with less impact on their family. So your definition of what constitutes part-time employment will have to be made within the context of your own family situation as well as the type of job you are considering.

That said, let's review the key reasons why mothers choose to work part time, examine creative ways in which they do so, and explore why sometimes it isn't always the best choice for you or your family.

Why Work Part Time?

What motivates women to seek part-time employment will be different for each family. Here are some of the primary reasons women work:

> *Financial Stability*—Some families simply can't make ends meet on one income. Despite cutbacks to their budget, they continue to fall further into the red. Working part time is a compromise that eases the financial stress on the family and, in some cases, provides a much-needed

benefits package that includes important perks such as group health insurance.

Preservation of Skills—With the rapid and dramatic changes that can occur in many career fields, especially in the sciences, some women choose to work part time to remain current in their profession. Colleen, a chemist and mother of three who has since returned to full-time work, wishes that she had had the opportunity to work part time when her children were younger:

I found it difficult to return to a highly technical field after being away for 14 years. Technology had changed drastically in that time period, resulting in sophisticated instrumentation and applications that I had no opportunity to use or learn previously. Going back to school in my forties was necessary to be on an equal performing level with my colleagues.

Career Retention—Certain jobs can be difficult to acquire. Some women are able to reduce their hours and retain their employment status at their firms, making it easier to return to a full-time career later. Beth, an accountant and mother of two, chose to work part time to remain up-to-date with accounting and tax laws which change frequently. As Beth says, "It keeps my options open at the firm and might even lead to a promotion at a later date."

Avoiding Pitfalls—If a spouse's job status is unpredictable or the marriage rocky, some women may decide to work part time. In the event that the unfortunate happens, they will be in a better position to quickly return to full-time status and maintain some financial stability. This is why Cheryl, a legal assistant and mother of three, accepted a part-time contracting job:

When I agreed to go back to work part time, I found that I liked the flexible hours, and I really enjoyed having the income again. I also wanted to get my foot back in the door. At the time, there were issues in my marriage that made me realize how important it was to be self-sufficient.

Retaining a Sense of Self—There is no question that staying at home can be a self-esteem zapper for many women. Working part time can help remind a woman of her unique capabilities, keep her intellectually challenged, provide a place where she can engage with other professionals, and supply her with an independent source of income for both herself and for her contribution to the household. Kim, an artist and mother of two, continues to perform part time freelance work from home. Here's her take:

Ever talk to a thirty-year veteran stay-at-home mom? It can be so boring. My husband's mother just never seemed to recover from staying at home for so many years. She let her own interests die on the vine. Her kids have been gone for almost twenty years, and yet she still can't find the time to do anything fun for herself. She's too busy doing housework and tending to the needs of her husband and pets.

Now, don't get me wrong, she's an incredible source of information. She can cook anything or fix any stain on any clothing or carpet. Being at home myself has given me a new appreciation of her many skills. But I don't really want to be like her. I love my family, but staying home with my kids is just a temporary gig. Even if I never go back to the corporate world, you won't catch me lost and miserable when my darling babies grow up and leave home.

How Do They Work?

The ways in which women work are only limited by their imagination. More and more companies are realizing the benefits that come with flexible work options. Part-time work is only one of the alternatives offered by many firms. Here are some examples of the different ways companies are creating flexible workplaces:

Flexiplace or Telecommuting—Sometimes referred to as the virtual office, this permits employees to work at an alternative, and more convenient, worksite such as their home.

Job Sharing—Two people share a single job, with the salary and benefits prorated accordingly.

Voluntary Reduced Time—Employees are permitted to reduce their work hours for a specific period.

Hours Averaging—In this method, employer and employee agree on a set number of hours per year and then design a schedule that works for both parties.

I like to refer to those who work part time as "hybrids." I consider myself a hybrid. In the 10 years that I've been home, I have written several books, have been employed part time on the weekends at psychiatric hospitals, and taught an occasional psychology class during the evenings. I generally look for work that I can fit around my husband's full-time schedule and that requires, at most, only occasional child care for short periods.

I recently received a call from a local college asking if I'd be interested in teaching a psychology class two nights each week. It's the perfect job for me because it doesn't require child care and doesn't interfere with my children's or my husband's schedule. We could use the extra income, so I accepted the position.

My children's pediatrician is also a hybrid. She is a mother of three young children and only works three days a week, from 9 am to 12 noon. Despite her currently limited hours, she remains a well-respected doctor. Mothers like me, who understand the value of her time at home and appreciate what she is doing for her family, are happy to work around her schedule.

Our family dentist is a single mother who operates her own practice. Because she has no spouse to support her, giving up her business wasn't an option. But putting her son into full-time child care wasn't an acceptable option for her either. So she converted an extra room at her office into a play area and has her staff help her care for her son during business hours. I recently arrived for an appointment and was delighted to see my dentist sitting outside on a bench with her son in her lap. Accommodating her son in this manner had to have its challenges, but those moments "on the bench" must make it all worthwhile.

A nurse told me once about a pair of married doctors she worked for who took turns being stay-at home parents. Every two years, they'd switch roles from doctor to stay-at-home parent. In this innovative way, they shared clientele, maintained their practice, and, most important, made sure one parent was always home taking care of the children.

Beth, the accountant and mother of two, found a nanny whom she shares with another mom. To pull this off, she had to find a part-time working mother willing to synchronize schedules as well as a flexible sitter who would provide services to two different homes.

Part-Time Employment Isn't for Everyone

Part-time work is certainly not the best answer for some mothers. I acknowledged earlier that part-time employment can be stressful for many families. It can add unnecessary hassle to an already demanding life with little children. Deborah, a college art professor and mother of two, told me of an interview she had recently that perfectly illustrates the anxiety associated with working:

> Today, I went to my first job interview in four years. I even ironed a blouse (burning my fingers as I was putting the iron away) and found a matching bead necklace so that I would look professional.
>
> So how did the interview go? We had a very nice chat, and it was clear to both of us that I was plenty qualified. But did I want to take the job? This is where it gets sticky for me, because I am not sure I do.
>
> There are so many factors to mom working. There are the issues of schedules, the kids, the animals, and the house. I am already overwhelmed by the daily minutiae that must be taken care of just to keep the ship steering clear in the channel. The thought of adding the demands of a part-time job to the mix makes my hands sweat.
>
> So, I realized during the interview, while sitting across from this very nice man for whom I would clearly enjoy working, that this probably was not the time to take on another commitment. The extra $100 a week that I'd earn for this part-time position would have to go to therapy bills if I added one more thing to my plate.

It can also be difficult finding quality part-time child care. The better centers, those that do more than just baby sit, want full-time children so they can ensure that they have the income to pay for their full-time staff. Part-time children block their ability to fill their limited slots and, ultimately, reduce their income. You might consider sharing a slot, or paying for a full-time slot that you use only part time, but be aware that many centers may view this as a disruption to their program and forbid it.

Working part time outside of the home has other challenges. Consider the amount of time it takes to get ready in the morning. You need to feed and bathe your child, gather baby supplies, and get yourself dressed and fed, all before you can even step out the front door. If you don't have a sitter who comes to your home, you'll have to drop your baby off on your way to work. That can add up to a lot of effort for just a few hours of work at the office.

Working part time doesn't necessarily give you that sense of importance you had when you worked full time, either. In fact, it may be just the opposite. I was employed on weekends for a private children's psychiatric hospital and came in one Saturday to find that the facility had closed the unit I was working in. Nobody thought it important enough to call the weekend therapist and let me know I was out of a job.

Working limited hours as a therapist also gave me the sense of being an outsider. I often felt that I was not privy to what was going on internally at the hospital. I sort of hung awkwardly somewhere between stay-at-home mom and career mom. I also found it difficult at times to switch gears and mentally jump from making play dough in the morning to treating psychiatric disorders in the afternoon.

Important Considerations

If you are contemplating part-time work, you should carefully consider four factors before accepting the job.

> *Your Spouse*—Are you pondering working part time around your husband's schedule? This may help alleviate the problem of day care but will likely add more stress

to your husband's workweek. Consider his schedule. Will he be coming home from a difficult job, tired and in need of some downtime? How is your husband's personality and temperament? Is he easygoing around the kids at the beginning or the end of a long day? Does your husband support your endeavor, and is he up for the added challenge? Before you make any decision, talk it through to make sure you both understand the potential repercussions of your decision.

Your Children—How many children do you have, and what are their ages? What type of child care would be required, and what is actually available in your area? Can you set your work schedule to be at home during most of your children's waking hours?

Your Career—Sometimes the jobs available to you as a stay-at-home mom aren't the same ones that will advance your career. Because my line of work as a therapist is very stressful, I have often fantasized about working a few hours each week at a low-stress job like, say, a Lancôme cosmetics counter at a plush department store. While this and other oddball ideas I've had sound like they could be a lot of fun, I've ultimately decided against them. My resume is already somewhat disjointed by my stay-at-home years. So, I'm selective in choosing part-time work to help keep some semblance of continuity on my job record.

You—Are you up for this? Raising children, especially young babies, can be very challenging. Nonstop feedings, sleepless nights, and wacky hormones can take their toll on a mother. Is this really the best time to begin part-time work?

Would it be better for you to first get used to the new addition to your family?

Part-time employment is definitely not for everyone, but for many women, it can provide something more tangible than a paycheck. It can give you a break from the home, keep you connected to other professionals, and give your self-esteem a needed boost. But unless your basic needs are not otherwise being met, you should never feel as though you must work. If you are content, financially or otherwise, then consider sitting back and just enjoying the ride.

Working from Home

Working from home can solve a number of problems otherwise associated with the hassles of working part time outside of the home. Most important, you are better able to work around your children's schedule and minimize disruptions to your home life.

Some companies, as I mentioned earlier, offer "flexiplace" or "telecommuting," where employees can continue to perform their jobs from home. I have a neighbor, also a mother, who continues to work part time out of the house as a marketing consultant. Other professions, such as those involving the arts, writing, accounting, or editing, are also relatively easy to adapt to the home.

A wonderful benefit of working from home or running a home-based business is that you incur fewer expenses because your need for child care, fancy clothes, and gasoline is lower. And, often, the expenses that are incurred are tax-deductible.

Direct Marketing

When more traditional options for working from home are limited, many women look for alternatives outside of their career field. A very popular option is to sign on as a consultant for a direct marketing company. This type of work usually involves sales of items such as candles, makeup, jewelry, toys, cookware, and other items targeted at women and children.

Often, direct marketing companies use sales "parties" to attract new customers and recruit additional consultants. (If you haven't been invited to such a party yet, you undoubtedly will be.) As much as many despise the thought of selling, most women often find the parties to be a lot of fun. Not only do they offer an opportunity to shop, they are also a great excuse for women to get together. Here's what Tammy, a former quality assurance auditor, has to say about her new job:

> I am currently an independent consultant and I love it. It involves more work than I originally thought it would, but I get to socialize and make money at the same time. I work in the evenings, but never more than three nights each week. Having the freedom to choose when I work has been the best part. My daughter loves to help and has told me that she wants to be a consultant when she grows up. I have met some amazing women who started as my customers and then became my friends.

Jenny, a special education teacher and mother of five, has this to say about her former home-based business: "I did very well, and it made more money than either my husband or I had expected. It was great. I was able to get out of the house a couple of nights each week, and I felt like I was accomplishing something while doing what I really enjoyed."

But working from home is not as easy as it may seem. For one thing, it can be very difficult to concentrate with children hanging on your legs. Though I consider writing to be a great stay-at-home job, I am also up to wee hours of the morning trying to meet deadlines because of the unending disruptions during the day.

Many of the catalogs for home businesses showcase a well-dressed mother working at her computer while her very patient child sits happily on her knee. What they don't show is the scene two seconds later when the kid knocks mom's coffee onto her keyboard. The reality is that when you work from home, you work very hard.

Although Tammy has found her business rewarding, it has been challenging, too:

> There is a lot of follow-up work involved that I did not originally anticipate. I am very organizationally challenged, so setting up a system that works for all the information I need to keep track of has been a trip. The tidiness of my house has suffered. The hardest part has been setting "office hours" and sticking to them. It takes discipline to stay at my desk rather than throw in a load of laundry, run the vacuum, take a nap, watch soaps, or go out to lunch with my mom. I am very easily distracted, so that has been a struggle.

Two words of caution. There are many unscrupulous businesses out there, so do your research before signing up. Assure yourself that the marketing company and its agents are reputable. Also, you may find that the marketing firm encourages you to view friends and family as potential customers. Be careful to keep your business and your acquaintances separated in your mind. Something is amiss when you start viewing your friends and family as a way to fill your pocketbook.

Returning to Full-Time Work—A Reality Check

Making the decision to return to work can be complicated and confusing. When is the best time to do so? Should you work full time or part time? As your child approaches school age, many of you will begin to struggle with these questions.

I share your dilemma. In three years, my youngest will begin kindergarten. What will I do? Originally, I assumed I'd get on with the business of restoring my career. But now that I have three children in elementary school, I can see that my initial plan was flawed. I didn't take into consideration the question of who would be home with the kids during Christmas, Easter, and summer vacations. I also failed to factor in how often children become sick and need to stay home from school.

I am also keenly aware that my career has been on hold these past 10 years. While my part-time employment has helped to make my eventual reentry into the full-time workforce easier, it has done little to push my career forward. When I left NASA over 12 years ago, I was earning more, on a per hour basis, than what I earned earlier this year at my part-time job as a therapist. While my husband's income on a per-hour basis has outpaced inflation over the years, mine hasn't even remotely kept stride. So, when we return to our jobs, we will likely return to where we left off, not where we would be had we retained our employment.

I've Seen Too Much

Because I originally assumed that I would eventually go back to work full-time once all my children were attending school, I made a point to observe the activities of summertime and after-school child care programs whenever possible. What I've seen hasn't impressed me. Caregivers generally appear to be undereducated, and many programs are overcrowded with unmanageable kids.

One afternoon, I took my children to the playground at a nearby elementary school. There was another child, who looked to be in kindergarten, playing on the equipment when we arrived. I looked around for his parents, but saw no one. I thought this strange because the child was too young to be unsupervised. He played with my children for at least 15 minutes before an angry woman appeared from behind the school building and hollered, "There you are!" The child was attending the after-school program, and it had taken the instructors that long to notice he was missing and to find him. In the meantime, the child could have wandered away or been picked up by a stranger.

In the years I've been at home, my family has lived in several different locales. I've noticed a common tendency of working parents to leave their young children alone to roam, unsupervised, for hours on end. I've witnessed underage youth drinking beer and smoking dope on their own front lawn, kids arriving home in the middle of a school day with groups of friends, and, of course, parties while the parents are out of town. I sometimes wonder if the parents know their children as well as their neighbors do.

I Know Too Much

An acquaintance once asked me if I remembered what it was like to be a child. Yeah, I sure do. That's why I want to be around to ensure the same things don't happen in our home! It is my firsthand experience, combined with what I've learned as a therapist, that makes it hard for me to pretend that going back to work full time wouldn't be detrimental to my family in some way.

Colleen, the chemist and mother of three, was home for 14 years before she returned to work full time. Her children have since left the nest. In hindsight, she now regrets that she wasn't able to stay home when her children were teenagers: "I could never imagine dropping them off at day care when they were small, but if I had known that I could have been home during the teen years instead, I think I would have done it all in reverse."

In reverse? Is she suggesting that we are approaching it all wrong? No. Her point is that she is now able to see that she was also needed during her children's turbulent teenage years. Maybe even more so. Hers is not an isolated opinion either. Michelle, the veterinarian and mother of three, left her part-time work to become a full-time mother when her daughters grew older. Here's why: "As our children became teenagers, it seemed they needed me even more than when they were younger. That's when I decided to stop working part time altogether. It was a very positive move for our family."

Today, there is a growing body of research to back the observations of Colleen and Michelle. According to the nonprofit research group, Child Trends, when children approaching age 13 are regularly unsupervised or cared for by siblings, they are at increased risk for accidents, developmental problems, social and behavioral problems, and academic achievement and school adjustment problems.

With all of life's hectic demands, family meals have nearly become a thing of the past. Finding time for a traditional sit-down meal can be even more difficult to achieve when both parents work full time. Dr. Dianne Neumark-Sztainer's research showed that those who regularly ate meals in a positive structured environment were less likely to show signs of an eating disorder, including chronic dieting, use of diet pills, and vomiting. Of those girls who ate one or two family meals each week, 18 percent showed signs of an eating disorder. This is compared to only 9 percent of girls who ate family meals three to four times a week, and this percentage was even lower when they ate five meals a week as a family. Boys also benefited from family meals, but the association was not as strong.

The National Longitudinal Study of Adolescent Health interviewed more than 3,000 pairs of mothers and their teens and reported that teenagers are less likely to start having sex when their mothers are involved in their lives. Their research also reveals that simply warning teenagers about the dangers of sex or telling them that they shouldn't have sex doesn't stop them from becoming sexually active .

It is especially disturbing to me that parents would leave their children alone and unattended for long periods. The world today is more dangerous than it was when we were growing up. Teen sex isn't just about unwanted pregnancies anymore. It can mean death by AIDS. The types of drugs that are now available to young children are much stronger and more addictive than they were when we were younger. The Internet has brought strangers into the home and taken our children into a world of perversion. Research indicates that one in five children has been sexually solicited online, and one in four has been sent a picture of a nude person.

Don't Toss the Bunny Slippers Just Yet

It's been 10 years, and I still miss my career, the challenge, the income, and my coworkers. There are days when I wish that day care, after- and before-school child care programs, long hours in front of the TV, decreased supervision, and frequent dinners of cereal would actually be a good thing for my children. Often are the moments when I'd like to see all of the research disappear so I could go back to work full-time without a guilt trip.

But, despite this, I choose not to. I will not bury my head in the sand, paying no heed to the collective message that I've read, seen, and experienced. The job of parenting is much too important and its consequences too far reaching for me to do so.

The hard work of parenting doesn't end when our children start kindergarten. The research tells us that our influence as mothers remains important long into their teen years. Some of us, initially unable to reconcile our career with our home life, will eventually come to accept the need to set aside our career for a longer period than we originally anticipated. Others will find a way to balance their family needs and a limited career.

Whichever direction you choose, always keep the best interests of your children front and center. Don't squander the hard work and sacrifice you've invested during your children's early years. And never forget that they need you for *all* stages of their young lives.

Final Thoughts

*The real voyage of discovery consists
not in seeking new landscapes, but in
having a new eye.*

~Marcel Proust

It is the summer of 2005. Nine days ago, monstrous Hurricane Katrina devoured much of the Gulf Coast. The dead have yet to be counted. In areas hardest hit, you can no longer tell the difference between the wealthy and impoverished as entire towns have instantly joined ranks with the latter. Homes, both large and small, all look the same now. They are piles of rubble.

Like many, my mind struggles to comprehend the magnitude of the loss. Entire communities have been destroyed. Homes, jobs, and loved ones have been washed away with the floodwaters. Among the incomprehensible, an image has been imprinted in my mind. It is the picture of an elderly woman sitting in a rocker on what is left of her front porch. She gazes numbly outward, past her rubble-strewn home of 60 years, to a place in her mind known only to her. She is alive; but her life, as she once knew it, is gone.

Interviews with survivors are naturally filled with grief, anger, and hopelessness. Yet, oddly enough, there are many among them who call themselves blessed. "Blessed?" reporters will ask. "But you have lost everything. How can you call yourself blessed?" Their response is always the same. "I still have my family."

In a world consumed by money, power, and status, it can take a disaster of this magnitude to peel away the fog and remind us of what is truly important in our lives.

In a few short years, my youngest will start school, following in the footsteps of his three siblings. When I eventually consider returning to work, I also must acknowledge that my career has suffered. Yet, while this time at home may never find a place on my resume, I will always recall it as my most important work.

I am indeed truly blessed.